Ag

When m
Julius M
ace dete
as their
Absalom
trouble is bound to follow. Is Swinging Susie, the singer at the Civic Banquet, really Smiling Sandra Smith, ruthless criminal? Is Inspector Lispington from Scotland Yard chasing Scott and Mosca or MacSnuff and Nick? Can Agaton Sax trap the real criminals? There is a lot of fun, and much excitement too, before the puzzle is solved.

Nils-Olof Franzén was head of Swedish radio, and he originally wrote the Agaton Sax stories to please his son. They were first published in Sweden in the 1960s, and have since found enormous popularity in both Europe and America. Another story about the great detective, *Agaton Sax and the Scotland Yard Mystery*, is also published by Beaver.

AGATON SAX

and the Criminal Doubles

Nils-Olof Franzén

Illustrated by Quentin Blake

Beaver Books

A Beaver Book

Published by Arrow Publications
17–21 Conway Street, London W1P 6JD

A division of the Hutchinson Publishing Group
London Melbourne Sydney Auckland Johannesburg
and agencies throughout the world

First published in Great Britain in 1971
Beaver edition 1984

Set in Linoterm Baskerville
by JH Graphics Limited, Reading

Printed and bound in Great Britain by
Anchor Brendon Limited, Tiptree, Essex

ISBN 0 09 935930 8

Contents

1

Unwelcome visitors

Oh, what a wonderful morning!

Oh, what a beautiful day!

In the little Swedish town of Bykoping it was the finest September day anyone could remember. The sun was shining from a cloudless sky. The air was warm and calm. In house after house people had stopped their cuckoo-clocks so that they could doze uninterrupted through the peaceful afternoon.

The railway station, too, basked in the sunshine. Mr Trainsley, the station master, had fallen asleep in his green rocking-chair, and was snoring happily, his face covered by a copy of Agaton Sax's superbly produced newspaper, the *Bykoping Post – First with the News – The Smallest Paper – but the Best.*

Mr Trainsley was waiting for the arrival of Train 3745 from Stockholm, unaware of what was waiting for him just round the corner. Unaware that the calm of the town was about to be shattered by two dreadful travellers, travellers who were at that moment passengers on Train 3745, and whose destination was Bykoping.

If you, dear reader, with your percipient eye, had seen them sitting there, you would certainly have cried aloud: 'Bless my soul! They can only be high-ranking international crooks.'

Why then didn't the guard, or the assistant

guard, or the engine driver notice what you would have noticed and express their alarm in the same way? The only explanation is that when they boarded the train in Stockholm, the two crooks wore false moustaches, which they took off a few minutes later because of the heat in the train.

If indeed they were crooks. . . .

They were sitting in the corner seats by the window. Suddenly one of them stretched out his hand for his mackintosh, which was hanging on a peg behind him. He took a map of the world from one of the pockets, opened it out and, pointing to a minute dot, said in English:

'We are approaching Bykoping now. We'll be there in seven minutes.'

The other man did not answer. He was staring out of the window, but he didn't seem to be looking at the scenery or enjoying the view as the train sped through Bykoping's delightful suburbs.

It was evident that these two men had undertaken a most important mission, in fact they looked so thoughtful they could easily have been on the most fateful journey of their lives.

'Next stop Bykoping,' the guard called out.

The two men gave a start. Was it their bad consciences that made them jump?

They stood up, took their battered, travel-stained suitcases from the luggage-rack and slowly walked out into the corridor.

They were the only people who left the train at Bykoping. As they stepped on to the platform they took a good look at Mr Trainsley, who had woken up and was ready, flag in hand, to wave the train off. They entered the Railway Restaurant and sat down at a table. The man with the map of the world spread it out on the cloth.

'Where are we?' the other man asked.

'Here,' said the man with the map, pointing at a small dot.

But his companion, having asked the question, seemed to lose interest. He fished a small dictionary out of one of his pockets and placed it on the table. As the waiter came up to them, politely asking what they wished to order, the man with the dictionary waved his right arm in a sweeping gesture, and said in very bad Swedish,

'A couple of minced oxen, I pray of you. Very much minced oxen – you have that, yes?'

'Minced oxen, sir?' asked the bewildered waiter.

'Yes, a couple of minced oxen, pray. Or

perhaps have you a couple of roast oxen, yes? No?'

The other man, realising that his friend was incapable of making himself understood, gave him a withering look, and, turning to the waiter, spoke a few words. He knew very little more Swedish than his friend, but somehow he managed to make the waiter understand what he wanted.

'No, not oxen, not at all – completely wrong. My friend has read the menu wrong. There are peas here? Green peas, yes? Most good, yes. Two green peas, yes! In soup, yes. And porks in soup, yes. Most good.'

When at last they got their plates of pea soup they ate voraciously. They probably hadn't had anything to eat since leaving London forty-seven hours earlier. They finished their meal without saying a word.

Having paid for their food, they strolled into the deserted High Street and walked slowly down the middle of the road. A trained observer would have spotted the characteristic bulges in their right hip pockets that indicated they were carrying revolvers.

Without doubt the same trained observer would have felt his blood run cold if he had looked first at the two men, and then at a large poster on the notice board of the Police Station at the end of the High Street.

WANTED

The World's most dangerous international gangsters
JULIUS MOSCA and OCTOPUS SCOTT
are at large again.

Working as a team, they boss the world of Crime!
They must never be trifled with!
They must be seized at once, by anyone who finds them, anywhere.

Julius Mosca

Octopus Scott

They are masters in the art of disguise, but they must be unmasked.
Any clue, however small, will be treated as important by the Police!
Report anything suspicious immediately either to Scotland Yard or to Agaton Sax!
DON'T THINK ABOUT IT. DO IT NOW!
A REWARD is offered for any information leading to the arrest of Julius Mosca and Octopus Scott.
For further information, apply to:

The Bykoping Police
(signed)
Antonsson
Sergeant

If you compared the portraits on the poster with the two men now walking slowly and deliberately down the otherwise empty High Street – how could you doubt their identity? These two men could only be Julius Mosca and Octopus Scott.

In the Police Station, Sergeant Antonsson was, as usual, filling up forms. He was just writing a report on three cornets which he had found abandoned on the pavement in East Street.

He looked up from Form 5A, the fourth column of which he had just filled in, and saw that the Station clock said 15.27.

Antonsson put down his pencil. What strange impulse was it that made him choose this particular moment to rise from his chair, stretch himself, and walk slowly towards the door? He opened the door and went out into the welcoming sunlight. A little fly hummed past his right cheek. He stretched again and yawned.

Suddenly his yawn was transformed into a horrified stare, his expression froze in a mixture of awe and terror as he caught sight of the two men. For a few seconds he stood motionless, his mouth open, his arms stretched above his long, narrow head.

Slowly, deliberately, the two men approached. The glare from the ice-cold eyes chilled the sunlight that up till then had warmed the quiet High Street.

Several thousand thoughts chased each other round Antonsson's brain. Then, with an enormous effort, he shook off the horror that had paralysed him and rushed back into his office. He flung himself at the telephone, and with trembling forefinger dialled a three-figure number, the number of the *Bykoping Post*. He needed to talk to Agaton Sax.

Agaton Sax was sitting at the desk in his editorial office in the High Street, not very far from the Police Station. In his hand he was holding his magnificent editorial telescope.

The ringing of the telephone broke the silence in the room. He lifted the receiver.

'Hallo,' he said.

'Agaton Sax?'

'Speaking.'

'It's the police. Help!'

'Yes, I know. Don't be afraid!'

'But they are here!'

'I know.'

'What am I to do?'

'Nothing.'

'But they are coming towards the Police Station. Suppose they see the poster? They will be terribly angry.'

'Then lock the door.'

'But suppose that doesn't do any good?'

'*Lock the door*. Now, while I hold on.'

Antonsson had no choice but to obey orders. He made a dash for the door and turned the key in the lock. Running back to the telephone, he shouted down the mouthpiece:

'Hallo!'

'Stay where you are,' Agaton Sax ordered, 'there is no need to panic. I have been watching them all the time. I can see them through my editorial telescope.'

'But what can we do? Why on earth have they come to Bykoping? What have they got against *me*?' Antonsson cried in despair.

'Listen carefully, Antonsson. You are to do absolutely nothing without asking me first! Leave the receiver off your phone so that you remain connected to my office, and I will give you all the necessary orders. Then everything will go smoothly.'

Antonsson nodded, then cautiously put his head out of the window. He saw that the two crooks were approaching the Police Station, step by step, and nothing could stop them.

Agaton Sax laid the receiver down on the desk and pressed his editorial telescope once again to his right eye. The expression of grim determination on his face would have frightened anyone who saw it. But nothing could frighten him. With the utmost concentration he watched the two men in the street. Suddenly he gave a low whistle, leaned back in his editorial chair and, gently smoothing his elegant moustache, murmured:

'Aha! This is it!'

He seized the telescope again. The two men had now reached the Police Station. One of them suddenly tugged the other's sleeve and, pointing at the poster, shook his fist and shouted something Agaton Sax could not quite hear. He was obviously furious – just as Antonsson had thought he would be.

The other man did not answer. His face was cold, expressionless and spine-chilling. He put down his suitcase, raised his right arm and tore down the poster.

Antonsson saw it all. He quivered.

'What do I do now?' he shouted down the telephone.

'Nothing.'

The two men on the pavement looked up and down the street, as if searching for something. Then the one with the map of the world opened it out again. This time, after examining it carefully through a magnifying-glass, he pointed at the offices of the *Bykoping Post*.

They crossed the street. It was quite clear that they were following a carefully worked out plan of action. There was never any hesitation about anything they did.

They reached the entrance to the *Bykoping Post* and paused for a moment, apparently deciding whether it would be better to enter the building by the main entrance in the High Street, or walk round to the back.

For the first time they seemed to wonder what to do next. Could it be that now the moment of decision had come their spirits were beginning to flag?

At that moment a voice was heard, a voice of authority. It was difficult to say where the voice came from, there was no one in sight. Did it come from the keyhole? Or from the lamp hanging over the front door? Or from the rose-bush growing on the right-hand side of the door? The invisible voice spoke impeccable English. It said:

'Please come in, gentlemen. Agaton Sax is expecting you. You will receive further instructions as you enter the hall.'

The two men jumped and looked at each other anxiously.

Then, silently, they opened the door.

2

Truth is stranger than fiction

Aunt Matilda went out shopping at 15.10. Agaton Sax was very particular about food and drink, so it was on his instructions that she went first to Svensson's General Store. At Svensson's you could buy the best chicken liver in town, the freshest celery, spiciest soy sauce and so on. After that she visited Mrs Elsa-Lotta Johansson, who had taken over her mother's haberdashery shop. The two were great friends and Mrs Elsa-Lotta Johansson always invited Aunt Matilda to coffee on Fridays. This was a Friday.

The compositor employed by Agaton Sax, who was also called Johansson, finished work at 15.00, and went home. So Agaton Sax was alone as the two men slowly walked up the stairs. He was standing by the window, and fingering a thick gold watch-chain which looped across his stomach from one waistcoat-pocket to another.

He was completely calm, which was to his credit, because he was playing an extremely risky game – so risky, indeed, that any ordinary person would have turned giddy at the thought of it.

But Agaton Sax had made a bet with himself, and the odds were 99.5 to 0.5 on his being the victor. The 0.5 he allowed to represent the remote possibility that he could have reached even one incorrect conclusion, enough to destroy the whole delicate fabric woven by his logical thought and analysis.

The door opened very slowly, and the two men entered the room. Agaton Sax did not move a muscle. With his usual unusual *sang-froid* he faced this peril as he had done so many others in the past.

'Please come in, Mr Julius Mosca and Mr Octopus Scott – because you are Mosca and Scott, aren't you?' he added sharply.

The two men did not answer. A pregnant silence filled the room.

'Please sit down,' Agaton Sax said.

The two men looked suspiciously at Agaton Sax, then glanced at each other, then sat down. Remaining by the window, Agaton Sax said:

'What is the nature of your business with me, gentlemen?'

Of course he knew very well the nature of their business with him, but he wanted to hear it from their own mouths. His voice was cold.

'We are being persecuted.'

'Persecuted? By whom?'

'By Scotland Yard.'

'And you have come to me for assistance?'

'You are a mind reader.'

'I am.'

This was indeed something new. Two giants in the World of International Crime coming to Agaton Sax to ask for protection from Scotland Yard. But Agaton Sax was not in the least surprised. On the contrary, at this very moment he realised triumphantly that there wasn't even a 0.5 per cent risk that he could be wrong. He was 100 per cent right.

That is why, suddenly, his whole attitude towards the two men changed. He picked up a dish of apples and passed it to them.

'Aunt Matilda picked them herself,' he explained affably. A few seconds later he added: 'I'm all ears, gentlemen.'

One of the men put his apple down and, looking Agaton Sax steadily in the eye, began his strange tale:

'My name is *not* Julius Mosca, nor am I the person who calls himself Julius Mosca, if you see what I mean. My name is, on the contrary, Absalom Nick, and what is still more important, I really *am* Absalom Nick. I am an ordinary honest poultry-farmer from Chickenchester, a small village to the south-west of London. I have always lived very peacefully with my chickens, doing no one any harm. I specialise in two breeds: the red-brown Huntingtonhampshire-South-east-Woosterhenpecker, and Plym.'

'Plym?'

'Yes, Plym. It all started with a Plym chicken. I

mean, this was how all this started – the whole nasty business. Two years ago I succeeded in hatching some three hundred Plym eggs. After a few weeks I noticed that one of the chickens lacked the brown spot on her crown that is the characteristic feature of this particular breed. As a result of this confusing and alarming discovery I rang up Professor Pendleton, who is one of the world's greatest experts on poultry. He was very interested in my story and asked me if I would be kind enough to come to his office at the Institute of Poultry Research, since he naturally wanted to have a look at my chicken. As we were arranging the time of my visit he remembered that he was due to come to London, and suggested we should meet somewhere in town, perhaps Regent's Park. If I brought my chicken along, we could have a look at it together. I put the chicken in a large brown hatbox – well, not quite brown, more yellow, dark yellow, I'd say. I took the Underground to Regent's Park, and went in, as we had agreed to meet just inside the gate. I sat down on a bench and put the hatbox on the ground at my feet. Now and then I lifted the lid of the box and peeped into it to see that Hercules – that was the chicken's name – was all right, and had enough air in his little round prison.'

Agaton Sax was listening intently. Small beads of sweat broke out on Mr Nick's broad forehead as he reached this crucial point in his strange tale.

'Please go on,' Agaton Sax said kindly.

'Right from the very moment that I sat down on the bench, I had a vague feeling that someone was watching me. I looked round, but saw no one. Yet I had a foreboding, a feeling that disaster was lurking in the air. I didn't know where, I didn't know how it would strike, but I did know it was there, I felt it in my bones. It was a great comfort to me that there was a policeman patrolling not far away. How mistaken I was! The next time I bent down to peep at little Hercules, I noticed that the policeman was watching me in a shifty, treacherous sort of way. I shut the lid again. The policeman was coming towards me, slowly and deliberately. I felt uneasy. Perhaps it was against the law to bring chickens into the park through that particular gate. I broke out in a cold sweat when this terrible idea entered my mind. Suppose they were going to fine me a thousand pounds or more? I turned away, pretending not to see the policeman, but he was now only a few yards away. Then he stopped right in front of me, his legs wide apart, and he said: "What have you got in that yellow hatbox of yours?"

'I told him the truth. He bent down in order to see for himself as I put my hand into the box to take Hercules out and show him. But Hercules got scared and flew out of my hands, alighting a few feet behind the policeman. He – Hercules, that is – was a very good runner, so it was only a matter of seconds before he was out of the Park and fluttering down the middle of the road, holding up the flow of traffic and causing a traffic jam that had spread over half London before the policemen, three more who had joined us, and I managed to catch him.

'By this time, the first policeman was furious. Panting with exhaustion he pointed at me and said to the other three: "I recognise this man!"

' "Of course you do," I said, "since we met only ten minutes ago when you started all this trouble by insisting that I open the lid of my hatbox."

' "Don't you recognise him?" the policeman asked again, taking no notice of me.

' "Yes, in a funny way I think I do," said one.

' "But who is he?" said another.

'"I am Absalom Nick," said I, and I was very angry indeed; tired and fed up with all this nonsense. But the first policeman refused to let me go, he just stood there, looking at me with that sly and treacherous eye of his and muttering something under his breath. Later I learned that his name was Scamp, and to my sorrow I was destined to see a great deal more of him. As you can imagine a large crowd had by this time gathered around us. I put Hercules back in the hatbox and was about to leave, when a voice from the crowd shouted:

'"Lor – look – isn't he the famous master criminal, Julius Mosca? They've nabbed him at last!"

'"Mosca! That's it!" said P.C. Scamp triumphantly. "Didn't I tell you I recognised his ugly mug from the photograph in the *Secret Code Register of Current Criminals*? You are under arrest, Julius Mosca, and whatever you say may be taken down and used in evidence, so don't say I haven't warned you!"

'In spite of my protests I was taken to the nearest police station. It was an hour before I was able to persuade the sergeant in charge to ring Scotland Yard. They told him that Julius Mosca was still in prison. After that they reluctantly let me go with a grudging apology. I returned to my chickens and nothing happened for a few weeks, but the very next time I was in London P.C. Scamp arrested me again, right in front of Buckingham Palace, a most disagreeable experience, I must say.

'Once again I was released, and returned to my chickens to pick up the threads of my former calm and happy life. But alas! How frail are man's hopes! How treacherous the sands on which he builds his castles in the air! On my next visit to London I stopped my car in Portland Place and got out to buy some pipe tobacco. No sooner had I put my foot on the pavement than two policemen rushed up to me, surrounded me, and arrested me. On arriving at the police station I learned to my horror that Julius Mosca had escaped from prison. After that, I was arrested at least twice a week, nearly always on Tuesdays and Fridays, the days on which I had to visit London. Certain places proved to be specially dangerous, for example, Underground stations, where there seemed to be particularly heavy concentrations of waiting detectives. Cinemas were also unsafe, since a surprisingly large number of plain-clothes detectives seemed to have the same taste in films as I did. Usually they waited until almost the end of the film and then tiptoed up to me and whispered that I had better come quietly so as not to disturb the rest of the audience. Another bad place was church, and as a regular church-goer I found it particularly revolting to be arrested just before the service began.

'For the first few weeks it took me an average of two hours to prove that I was not Julius Mosca. Later, however, every police station was issued with copies of Mosca's fingerprints and mine, so that the local police could easily establish my identity after arresting me. Scotland Yard's representative with whom I negotiated was a certain Chief Inspector Lispington, a man who, I assure you, never let up in his pursuit of Mosca. The agreement we reached was this. I was guaranteed compensation of one pound for every apprehension. The sum was to be sent to me by postal order the day after my arrest. However, even this carefully negotiated agreement proved to be unsatisfactory, since I was always arrested on entering the post office to draw my money. As long as I showed my postal order to the officers who arrested me, I was acquitted on the spot and did not have to go to the station for the usual fingerprint tests, but even so it was irritating. For apprehensions on post-office premises, I claimed compensation of eight shillings, but Inspector Lispington refused to pay more than six shillings on the grounds that these arrests lasted for only a very short time. After a year, I asked for a five per cent rise to cover the increase in the cost of living. I also claimed retrospective payment for all the arrests made prior to the agreement between Inspector Lispington and myself. I had claimed a retrospective payment from the very first, but they always refused to pay up. At this stage our negotiations lasted for over six weeks, and finally we came to terms, unsatisfactory from my point of view, but I did get a rise of six per cent. At about this time an official from the Ministry of Home Affairs wrote to me, suggesting that I assume a wig and a false beard. Scotland Yard, he told me, would of course be able to apply to the Ministry of Supply for a special consignment of free wigs and beards. He added that if I did not like the idea of wearing a wig and a false beard the authorities would be obliged if I would consider some other solution, such as wearing my hair cropped close to my head. But if I chose the latter course he felt it unlikely that the Ministry could offer me any special assistance. I absolutely rejected any suggestion that I should change my outward appearance. Alas, I would most certainly have accepted, had I been able to foresee what would happen only a few days later!'

Absalom Nick heaved a deep sigh, and turned his melancholy gaze on his companion.

Agaton Sax had listened to the whole story with the greatest attention, although he was not surprised by it, for experience had taught him that literally anything can happen in this world.

‘Please go on,’ he said in a low and sympathetic voice.

‘At that time I never imagined that one of the most disastrous days of my life was rapidly approaching. I refer to the day when I first met Mr Charlie MacSnuff.’

The other man nodded.

‘We are agreed, Mr Nick and I, that meeting each other was about the worst thing that could have happened to either of us,’ said Mr MacSnuff stoically. ‘Disastrous is the word, Mr Sax.’

‘I think you’d better take over now,’ said Mr Nick with a shrug.

‘As you wish, Mr Nick,’ said Mr MacSnuff. ‘Well, Mr Sax, as you have already guessed, my name is *not* Octopus Scott. My name is Charlie MacSnuff, and it is my bad luck to be as like Mr Octopus Scott as Mr Nick is like Julius Mosca. I am just an ordinary honest window-cleaner from Pimlico. I have a small firm, called *Charlie’s Window-Cleaning*, and my prices are moderate considering the excellence of my work. Here is my card, in case you would like to take advantage of my services at any time. Until eighteen months ago I never had anything to do with the police, never got mixed up with them at all, except that my sister’s husband’s sister was at one time engaged to a policeman who emigrated to Australia – but that was a long time ago, long before she – my sister’s husband’s sister, that is – married her present husband, so it hardly counts, does it? Well, one day last year, I had promised *Chocolate Cream Ltd.*, to clean their windows – you know, that’s the big office building in Mock Street. I was working, as usual, safely inside my big cage, which my assistant, Jack, operates with a pulley rigged up on the roof. When you clean windows you always start from the top, and Jack had lowered me as far as the eighth floor, when I saw a charming young lady sitting at her typewriter behind the window I was going to clean. I lifted my hat to her and she stared at me, then looked down, as if she wanted to check something in the newspaper she had propped up on her typewriter – this was during office hours, mind you, Mr Sax. She looked up again and stared hard once more at me, her eyes starting out of her head – then she screamed, my goodness me, how she screamed – I'll never forget it, though I've heard quite a few women scream in my life, I can tell you. After that she dashed out of the room, still screaming, and four or five minutes later the police arrived. They shook their fists at me and told me I had better come down, and not try any of my dirty tricks on them. Even Jack, my assistant, believed I was Octopus Scott when he saw the scoundrel's picture in the *Evening Yell* after work.

'So that's how it all started for me,' finished Mr MacSnuff, wiping his forehead with a large handkerchief. 'My resemblance to Octopus Scott is so uncanny that on some days the police got as many as twenty reports on my whereabouts, which meant at least one arrest a day. It became such a regular occurrence that I was tempted to try my hand at working out a few of the statistics of my case, and a sorry business it proved, I can tell you. During a period of fifteen months I was arrested every one hundred and third hour. I soon had to give up cleaning windows. I still ran the business, but Jack and Jim, my other assistant, had to do the actual work. Before circumstances actually forced me to give up I found I had had to turn down all offers of work from post offices, or houses near police stations. I also realised that school buildings were particularly dangerous spots for me, because the children immediately recognised me, and before I could say Jack Robinson I was surrounded by fifty or more brats who screamed and jeered and danced round me as if I were a guy on a bonfire. They would tie my hands and carry me in triumph through the streets to the nearest police station. I also learned that it was not safe for me to clean the windows of banks, for both bank clerks and their clients seem to be unusually suspicious. Fire insurance companies were another hazard. One day, I was cleaning the windows of *No Smoke Without Fire, Ltd.* I had disguised myself with a

fine false beard for this job, but unfortunately it got caught in a crack between two bricks and was ripped from my chin. Immediately someone shouted. "Octopus Scott is in the building – in disguise!"

'The worst of it was that Octopus Scott, the genuine one, was at large all the time. To my regret I was not as wise at Mr Nick, who had claimed compensation right from the start. I was eventually offered compensation for each arrest – but I never heard of such a thing as a rise of six per cent.'

'I think the reason for that is that I have been at the disposal of the police for about two years,' said Mr Nick bitterly, 'whereas you have so far served only about a year.'

'Anyway,' went on Mr MacSnuff, 'I, too, was destined to face a Day of Trial; the day, that is, when I met Mr Nick for the first time. That was when I plumbed the depths. It was a very fine afternoon. I had a couple of hours to spare, so I wandered into Hyde Park to think things over for a while. There was a man sitting beside me on the bench whom I had never seen before. After a little while he asked me if I had a match. I had. He lit his pipe then went on reading his newspaper. A few minutes later, however, he put down the paper, looked up, and said: "I say, the Police must be holding their Annual General Meeting here this afternoon, or perhaps the Massed Choirs of the Police Forces of Great Britain are assembling for a concert. Three thousand singing policemen. What a lark!'

'"Is that what you think, sir?" I said, looking round. I could see them, Mr Sax. There were hundreds of them – slowly encircling us, steadily drawing closer and closer. I got terribly angry. "O, no, sir," I said to the other man, "You are wrong. I know very well why they are here. Do you see seven black cars parked over there? They are Scotland Yard's special squad cars. Do you see those four men in dark suits standing under the lamp-post, looking grimly at us – or, rather at me? Do you see them, sir? They are detectives, take my word for it. Do you see that tall, limp, disagreeable-looking gentleman with a sad face and check trousers? Do you see him? Of course you do. He is Chief Inspector Lispington. As if I wouldn't recognise him anywhere! Do you know, sir, why all these policemen are closing in on us?"

'The other man, who was of course Mr Nick, had gone deadly pale. Clenching his fists with rage, he shouted furiously, "Yes, sir, I know! I know who they are! It's me they are after!"

'"You?" I exclaimed. "That's impossible! You don't mean to say that you are a dangerous criminal – not with a face like yours. I don't believe it!"

'"Just wait and see," he murmured, white with fury.

'A moment later, twenty policemen had surrounded us, and Chief Inspector Lispington approached. He looked at us solemnly for a moment or two without speaking, then he said: "The game is up, gentlemen! You'd better come quietly since you are under arrest!"

'Only an hour later did I fully realise the magnitude of the disaster which had fallen upon my innocent head. According to the most recent population survey, there are 7,863,820 persons living in London. By a stroke of unequalled bad luck, I had sat down on the same park bench as Mr Absalom Nick. You, Mr Sax, having such an expert knowledge of crime and criminals can easily imagine the consternation at Scotland Yard, when it was reported that Julius Mosca and Octopus Scott were sitting, side by side, on a bench in Hyde Park, doubtless plotting a joint undertaking far more terrible than anything either of them could have contrived alone.

'Even when our fingerprints proved irrefutably that we were ourselves they were reluctant to admit they had blundered again. We were questioned for more than three hours before being released – with the usual excuses and apologies.'

Mr MacSnuff wiped his forehead. His recollections were evidently most painful. Agaton Sax had been listening intently all the time.

'Extraordinary,' he murmured, deep in thought. 'And what happened next?' he added, leaning back in his chair.

'Well,' said Mr Absalom Nick, with a sigh, 'there was the incident of the box.'

'The box?' said Agaton Sax, pricking up his ears.

'Yes. The secret box. As a matter of fact, that's why we have come to you, Mr Sax.'

'I see. Tell me all about it!'

'One day last month,' said Absalom Nick, 'I was on my way home from London. As I was leaving the Underground at Uxbridge, a man suddenly approached me from behind. He touched my arm, and whispered: "I'm Lazy Bull, sir, if you remember. That's only my nickname, sir, if you permit me to remind you, sir. I was told to give you this gadget here, it's for you, sir, with regards from Uncle Teetotum, sir."

'I don't need to tell you, Mr Sax, that I have never in my life heard of anyone called Lazy Bull – nor do I have an uncle called Teetotum. I was very frightened by the stranger's mysterious words, partly because I felt sure that he wasn't one of the plain-clothes detectives from Scotland Yard who plagued my life. I decided to keep on talking to him and see what I could find out.

'"What gadget are you talking about?" I asked the man.

'"The one that Uncle Teetotum borrowed from you, sir," he answered.

'I felt a shiver of fear running down my spine as I realised that even the members of Mosca's own gang were mistaking me for Mosca. Evidently this man had been waiting for Mosca – and I happened to arrive before him. My first impulse was to call for the police, but on second thoughts I decided not to, since if I did they would be sure to arrest me at once. So I pretended to be Mosca, and I whispered to the stranger: "I'd like to talk to you. Let's go behind the shoe-shine stand over there."

'He fished a small square parcel out of his raincoat pocket.

'"Where is Mosca?" I whispered urgently as I took the parcel.

'"Mosca, sir?"

'"Yes, where is he?"

'"But sir, you're Mosca, aren't you?" he said, and began to tremble like an aspen leaf.

'What a fool I had been. You see, Mr Sax, as soon as I realised that this strange man and his secret box could lead me to the real Mosca, I became obsessed with the thought that if only I could find him and carry him in triumph to Inspector Lispington, not only would this put an end to Scotland Yard's incessant persecution, but I myself could claim the reward of £10,000 offered to anyone who could apprehend Julius Mosca. This thought made me so excited that I forgot that to this strange man I *was* Mosca, and had to act as if I was. Thank Heavens, my presence of mind saved me in the nick of time.

'"Of course I'm Mosca, you fool," I said angrily. "I'm talking about Mosca the race-horse."

'"The race-horse, sir?"

'"Yes. Don't you know that I own a race-horse called Mosca, who wins every race he runs in."

'"No, sir, I know nothing," he said. "About horses, that is."

'"I see. Well, where's Uncle Teetotum?"

'"In the usual place, sir."

'Unfortunately I couldn't very well ask him any more questions, so I just nodded, and put the parcel in my pocket.

'"Anything further, sir?"

'"No."

'He disappeared, and I hurried home with the parcel. When I opened it, I saw that it contained a camera of some sort. Then I rang up Mr MacSnuff. He managed to get to me without being arrested, and we examined the camera together. It was then that we noticed to whom it belonged.'

'To whom it belonged?' Agaton Sax had a dangerous gleam in his eye.

'Yes. And that is why we've come to you, Mr Sax,' said Mr MacSnuff seriously. 'On the bottom of the camera was a small silver plate, on which were etched the words: *Designed and Owned by Agaton Sax*.'

Agaton Sax leapt to his feet, as if bitten by a snake.

'Have you still got it?' he shouted.

'Yes, Mr Sax. Mr MacSnuff and I were so fed up with Scotland Yard that we decided not to hand it over to them. We thought we'd rather give it straight to you – hoping, of course, that you, in return, would be kind enough to apprehend these two scoundrels, Scott and Mosca, and so put an end to our miseries.'

'Oh well done! Splendid reasoning,' said Agaton Sax.

He was so full of pride that he appeared even more rotund than usual, and indeed looked so like an inflated balloon as he strutted up and down the room that it seemed likely he might take off at any minute and float to the ceiling. However, he didn't, and was still standing firmly on the floor when he spoke again.

'Well done, indeed, gentlemen. And now, if you give me that camera, as you call it, I assure you that within a few days Scott and Mosca will be done for.'

Mr Nick reached for his suitcase. But just as he was about to open it, there was a sharp knock on the door, followed by a silence lasting some two seconds.

There was another knock – this time sharper, more ominous.

Then, violently, the door was flung open, and a man stood on the threshold. He was tall and limp, and he was wearing a check cloak.

'Mr Julius Mosca and Mr Octopus Scott – in the name of the law I declare that you are under arrest,' he said.

The man was Chief Inspector Joshua H. Lispington. Just behind him stood the Bykoping Police Force, represented by Sergeant Antonsson.

3

Mr MacSnuff drops a brick

'Welcome to Bykoping!' Agaton Sax greeted Lispington warmly, but received in exchange only a dignified handshake.

'I am delighted,' said Lispington pompously, 'that we have at last laid hands on these two arch villains. For too long they have frustrated all our efforts to catch up with them.'

'Delighted is the last thing you'll be when you've had our fingerprints taken!' interrupted Mr MacSnuff indignantly.

'Oh no,' replied Lispington confidently. 'Don't you realise that I have seen through you ever since you left for Bykoping? Do you really imagine that I would have followed you all the way to Sweden if I had thought you were Absalom Nick and Charlie MacSnuff? I don't want to boast, but do you really think you can fool *me* with such a simple trick – me, with thirty-five years' service on the permanent staff of the Metropolitan Police Force to my credit, and fourteen years as Chief Inspector at Scotland Yard! Oh no! I don't need to check on you! Why should I carry your fingerprints about with me? Or, for that matter, those of Scott and Mosca?'

'Just a minute, Mr Lispington!' said Agaton Sax. 'Won't you sit down? These two gentlemen will certainly not try to escape. Before we go any further, would you be kind enough to tell me where my photo-recorder is at the moment?'

'You know very well where it is,' said Lispington reproachfully. 'When you visited me last month, you were kind enough to lend it to Scotland Yard for six months.'

'So where is it now?'

'It's under lock and key in Basement No. 3, Entrance 3B.'

'You are absolutely positive that it hasn't been . . . er . . . borrowed from you by either Mosca or Scott?'

'What an absurd idea, Mr Sax. Why should you suspect anything of the kind?'

'And these two gentlemen, you wouldn't by any chance think it possible that they might have my photo-recorder?'

'Absolutely out of the question! These two *gentlemen*, as you call them, are Julius Mosca and Octopus Scott!'

Agaton Sax turned to Absalom Nick and pointed to the brown suitcase at his feet.

'Would you please show us the camera, Mr Nick?' he asked politely.

Absalom Nick knelt on the ground, the key in his right hand. There was a click as he turned the lock, then he opened the lid and took out a square brown parcel, the size of an ordinary brick. He tore off the paper. The four men stared, their eyes wide with amazement.

It *was* an ordinary brick.

Anyone who has ever been to the dentist and then had the wrong tooth pulled out can easily imagine Agaton Sax's feelings at this dreadful moment.

'My photo-recorder!' he exclaimed. 'Somebody has stolen the most remarkable invention in the development of the camera! Mr Lispington, you are now dealing with a truly serious crime.'

Lispington regarded him coolly. Then he took the brick, examined it, and put it on Agaton Sax's desk.

'I don't understand what you are talking about, I just don't understand. Here is a man who says he is *not* Julius Mosca, and who is supposed to have received a camera which I *know* is under lock and key in Scotland Yard, and to prove his statement he produces a *brick*! This is an intolerable situation and I do not intend to put up with it. If he weren't already under arrest, I would arrest him immediately.'

Lispington was very angry, so angry that he banged his fist down on the desk to emphasise his statement.

Agaton Sax turned to Mr MacSnuff. His voice was cold as he said:

'Mr MacSnuff, would you be so kind as to open *your* suitcase?'

'Of course, Mr Sax.'

Mr MacSnuff produced a key, and opened his suitcase. Then he jumped back, as if he had seen a viper inside.

'Good gracious!' he exclaimed. 'What on earth is this? I don't understand either. The camera is in my suitcase.'

Agaton Sax picked up the camera reverently, examined it with care, pressed a number of buttons, and then put it down on the desk. Lispington, white as a sheet, sank down in a chair.

'Basement No. 3,' Agaton Sax murmured. 'When I lent this camera to Scotland Yard, it was not my intention to have it stolen by Julius Mosca. But Mosca stole it from you. Fortunately, as you have just seen, it fell into Mr Nick's hands. But why did you take it from him, Mr MacSnuff – for you did take it, didn't you?'

He looked daggers at poor Mr MacSnuff, who immediately collapsed.

'I confess, Mr Sax,' he said humbly, 'I did. You see, I was furious with Mr Nick because he managed to get far more compensation than I did for being arrested. I just wanted to make him look a fool, that's all. When our train stopped at a wayside station, we got off to stretch our legs. Suddenly I caught sight of a brick lying on the platform, and as Mr Nick's suitcase wasn't locked, I opened it, took out the camera, and put the brick in its place. It was a nasty thing to do, I do realise that now, but I assure you that I intended to give the camera back after giving Mr Nick a bit of a fright. Please forgive me, Mr Nick and Mr Sax.'

Deeply affected by this confession, everyone shook everyone else by the hand.

'Am I to understand, Mr Lispington, that you have been shadowing these two gentlemen all the way from London to Bykoping?'

'I happened to be on the same train, that's all.'

'I saw him coming,' said Antonsson proudly, 'and brought him to you, Agaton, because English policemen are not allowed to arrest anyone in Sweden without my permission. That is without the permission of the Swedish police, which in this particular case happens to be me.'

Agaton Sax was pacing up and down, gazing at the floor. It was obvious that he was thinking powerful thoughts behind his domed, intellectual forehead. The others waited, on tenterhooks, not daring to break the silence. No one would have dared.

Suddenly Agaton Sax stopped, and holding up his right index finger, said: 'Mr Lispington! We shall need all our determination to solve this case. These two gentlemen are not, as you already know, Scott and Mosca. They are really Mr Nick and Mr MacSnuff, and I am going to ask them to help us in carrying out a glorious task. Remember, Mr Lispington, that this is the first time that Octopus Scott and Julius Mosca have worked together. They have buried the hatchet for one reason only – they realise that there is no future for them unless they can destroy *me*, Agaton Sax. The folly of their plan is obvious, but then they have no choice. It's me or them. I can assure you that the fight will be hard. That is why you must all be prepared to do just what I tell you. You can all help if you follow my instructions.'

'Whatever you say, Mr Sax,' said Mr Nick. 'But please tell me first, what sort of a gadget is this photo-recorder of yours?'

'A very good question,' said Agaton Sax approvingly. 'My photo-recorder is probably my most ingenious invention, and that's saying a lot. It's a combined camera and tape-recorder. Well, you may say, there's nothing so very remarkable about that, and you would be quite correct. But you see what makes my camera different is that it can also see through everything that gets in its way. It doesn't matter whether you have it hidden in your sports jacket, your overcoat or even in a life-jacket, you can use it no matter how deeply hidden it is. It has a sort of X-ray eye, you see. But marvellous as that is, it is not all. It has yet another outstandingly useful feature, it films only things actually happening. Suppose I press this button now, it will start filming and record all our movements and everything we say. But as soon as we stop talking and moving about, or if we all leave the room, the camera will stop at once. If, after a minute or two, somebody enters the room again, the camera will start by itself. And so on. Now, I hope, you understand how important this remarkable design of mine is.'

They all nodded, silent with admiration – Lispington a little less than the others, though. Agaton Sax was beginning to look like an inflated balloon again.

'And now, gentlemen,' he went on enthusiastically, 'let us see what my camera has managed to see for us during its visit to England. I forgot to tell you that it is also a micro camera, which means that you can use microfilm in it. Thus it can operate for more than three hours without needing a new film. Now, to work! Excuse me, gentlemen – I'll be back in a minute.'

He dashed off into a small dark room, where he took the film out of the camera, and inspected it with a specially designed magnifying glass.

Meanwhile, Inspector Lispington remained standing by the window, looking out over the small Central Square of Bykoping. He was deeply disappointed and annoyed. He had not been able to prove, as he had hoped, that Nick and MacSnuff were in fact Scott and Mosca. He was absolutely satisfied in his own mind that the two disagreeable characters sitting across the room from him were none other than the Kings of the Underworld he had sought so long. But how could he hope to convince his conceited and far too intelligent Swedish friend that it was he, not Lispington, who was totally and hopelessly mistaken?

Agaton Sax reappeared, a triumphant smile on his lips.

'Gentlemen!' he announced solemnly. 'The remarkable scenes I am now able to show you were actually filmed in Mosca's hide-out in Grub Street.'

He unrolled a white screen, seven foot by five, and hung it from a nail on the wall. Then he adjusted the projector he had brought in, and switched off the lights.

An atmosphere of almost unbearable tension filled the room. Lispington fidgeted nervously with a small piece of paper which he kept rolling between his fingers. It was a warrant of arrest. The two gangsters (or gangsters' doubles?) stared intently at the screen, cross-eyed with anticipation. Sergeant Antonsson stood by the door, stiff as a ramrod.

A whirring noise was heard. Agaton Sax had started the projector. First the screen was illuminated by a dazzlingly white light, then, suddenly, violently, the whiteness was replaced by a vicious face, a face that could belong to only one man, the infamous gang leader, Julius Mosca, a man who terrorised the police forces of numerous towns in numerous countries, who was sought, shadowed, pursued wherever he went, who was a threat to the peace of the whole Western world. A man feared by everybody, everybody except Agaton Sax, for a few years ago Agaton Sax had become the only man ever to run him to ground, and get him sent to prison.

Everyone in the room except Agaton Sax winced when they saw the terrible face – particularly Mr Absalom Nick, who for a moment thought he was looking at himself in a mirror.

Mosca leered at them from the screen, a cruel smile playing on his thin lips.

'This is a test,' he said, 'the result of which, a film, will be sent to that most faithful of villains, my friend Uncle Teetotum. Since he seems to think there is something fishy about this camera he will be allowed to have the first look at this top-secret piece of film. I . . . er . . . borrowed the camera from Scotland Yard, but it was originally designed and made by that nauseating, fat little sleuth, Agaton Sax, my most unpleasant enemy. This detestable man, who is a disgrace to us all, is unfortunately as dangerous as he is nasty; a double-dealing traitor who will be a threat to our existence as long as he remains free to operate against us.'

Agaton Sax appeared outwardly unmoved by this recital of insults, but inwardly he was almost at boiling-point. And yet, how marvellously satisfying it was to hear Mosca confess to being afraid of him.

At this point Mosca crashed his fist on the table.

'I'm not going to put up with this any longer,' he thundered. 'Even you, Uncle Teetotum, will realise how dangerous this man is when I tell you that the camera filming me now is hidden *behind* the books on my bookshelf. The camera can see right through two of my favourite volumes, *Seventy Years in the Service of Crime*, and *Some of the World's Thickest Prison Walls and How to Scale Them*. You must be wanting to know how I came to get hold of this extraordinary instrument. Well it was quite simple really, done in a few moments. I have some clever secret agents, you know, and they had informed me that Scotland Yard had some peculiar gadget locked away that could take pictures and films in some very special way. So I picked up the telephone and rang Lispington, the ill-famed Inspector of whom I'm sure you've heard in some disagreeable connection. You remember, he's the one who can't tell the difference between me and that goose-faced poultry-breeder, Absalom Nick.

'"Good morning to you, Mr Lispington," I said. "My name is Oscar – Julius Oscar. You have a gadget of some kind under lock and key – haven't you? A new invention?"

'"What are you talking about, Mr Oscar?" said Lispington, and I could tell he was in a funk.

'"Now don't you try to play the innocent, Mr Lispington," I said. "I happen to *know* you've got it. But you'd better look out, this is just a friendly warning, meant to help you. There are certain nasty people about who would like to have that precious invention of yours."

'"What do you mean?" Lispington said, and he was almost panting with fear.

'"I mean just what I said. This very minute, for example, there might easily be someone snooping around and trying to steal it from you. Look out! Keep your eyes skinned, Mister!"

'Then I put down the receiver. An hour earlier I had sent two of my assistants, French Jules and Ernest Fingers Dodge, to Scotland Yard. They were disguised as office cleaners. French Jules started to clean the corridor where Lispington works, and Ernest Fingers Dodge set to work near Inspector Briggs's office – Briggs is Lispington's second in command. I reckoned that as soon as Lispington got my message, he would dash off to tell Briggs, and they would go straight to the room where the secret camera was kept, so as to check that it was still there. And that's exactly what they did. French Jules and Ernest Fingers Dodge sneaked after them, and so I found out where the camera was. After that it was child's play to pinch it.'

Lispington's face, which had for some time been rather grey, now turned white. He leapt to his feet, and struck out at the monstrous face on the screen. Then he pulled himself together, and sank down in his chair again.

Unperturbed by this interruption Mosca went on with his show.

'And now, Uncle Teetotum, I'm sitting here, with the camera hidden behind the books. I'm expecting a guest to arrive at any minute, a most interesting guest, I can tell you. He has no idea that the camera is hidden beind the books. Nor can he hear it, for it operates silently. Our conversation will be filmed from beginning to end without his knowing it. Capital! I'll send the film and the camera to you. When you've seen it, send it back with the camera to me. Give it to Lazy Bull, who'll be waiting to hand it over to me at Uxbridge Station on Wednesday at 16.00 sharp. Is that clear?'

Julius Mosca's eyes narrowed into two slits as he leant back in his armchair, puffing away at a gigantic, £25 cigar. It was obvious to anyone watching this giant of the Underworld that he was thinking about something pretty big.

Agaton Sax was unperturbed. He knew that he, and no one else, was capable of dealing with this uncrowned King of Crime – or perhaps that title should be reserved for another man, Octopus Scott.

There came a knock on the door of Mosca's office. The master criminal knocked the ash off his cigar, stood up and, turning to the camera, that is, to Uncle Teetotum, said:

'Now, Uncle, you'll get the surprise of your life. Watch carefully as I open the door.'

Mosca went to the door. The camera registered every movement, every sound, however slight. Slowly he grasped the door handle, then opened the door.

Into the room walked Octopus Scott – Criminal Extraordinary, King Spider in the web of international intrigue. The two men, rivals for as long as either of them could remember, smiled coldly at each other, and then shook hands with as much warmth as you would get from two lumps of ice.

'You're welcome, Mr Scott,' said Mosca. 'I have never before had the honour of meeting you, but I recognise you, of course, from your photograph in the *Secret Code Register of Current Criminals.*'

'I'm glad to hear that you study that useful book; it's important to be able to recognise the few people who really matter in the world of crime,' answered Octopus Scott with an amiable smile. At the same time he glanced round the room to make sure that there were no traps or secret doors anywhere.

'Won't you sit down, Mr Scott?'

'Sure.'

'I would like to do business with you, Mr Scott.'

'With me?'

'Yes.'

'Very wise of you, Mr Mosca, since I organise more than half the criminal activity in the world – or, to be more correct, just under two-thirds of it,' Octopus Scott added with a wicked smile.

'Oh, you do, do you? That's a good one! You've certainly got a sense of humour, Mr Scott! You organise perhaps just one-third of it. I am behind at least sixty per cent.'

'Was it your intention to insult me with preposterous lies when you invited me here?' exploded Octopus Scott, leaping from his chair in what appeared to be a frenzy of fury. 'Your conduct, Mr Mosca, bears a striking resemblance to that of certain undesirable policemen.'

'Please compose yourself, Mr Scott! Let us try to control our tempers! Won't you sit down again? Let me come to the point at once. You have heard of two gentlemen called Absalom Nick and Charlie MacSnuff. Of course you have. Now what I want to tell you is they have both been arrested – *together*. You see what that means? So, I ask myself – why shouldn't we – you and I – I mean . . .'

'Get ourselves arrested, is that what you mean? Never, Mr Mosca! Over my dead body! They can arrest you if you like; I wouldn't mind at all, but they'll never get me, I can tell you.'

'Please, Mr Scott, you don't understand. I'm not talking about us getting arrested. Far from it. I was going to say that if Mr Nick and Mr MacSnuff have entered into partnership, why can't we?'

Octopus Scott looked at Julius Mosca, the expression in his eyes a mixture of hatred, fear, and contempt. Then he pressed his fingertips against each other, leant back in his chair, and said:

'Remember, Mr Mosca, that you and I are natural enemies!'

He bit a piece off the end of the cigar Mosca had offered him.

'But you are mistaken, Mr Scott!' said Mosca with an ingratiating smile. 'I can prove to you that you are wrong.'

'You think so, do you? Then tell me, Mr Mosca, why do you go to almost any lengths to stop me printing and distributing my forged thousand-pound notes?'

'Simply because your printing-press is rotten! You are exposing *all* of us to the most terrible risks, don't you realise that? One fine day I, Julius Mosca, may be arrested for distributing counterfeit notes for which you are responsible! Would you call that fair play?'

'I'd call it jolly funny.'

'I see nothing funny in it,' exclaimed Julus Mosca, crimson with rage. 'Pick your words more carefully, sir!'

'Pick them yourself, sir.'

'The pears I bought at Johansson's are rotten to the core.'

4

Agaton Sax keeps calm and makes plans

Everybody jumped as the strangely meaningless words interrupted the film they were watching so intently. Everybody except Mr Sax, who realised at once that the voice belonged to Aunt Matilda, sending him a message through the speaking-tube that connected her kitchen with his editorial office.

'There's nothing to worry about, gentlemen,' he said, quickly disconnecting the tube.

Attention turned to the screen again. The skirmish which had begun before Aunt Matilda's interruption had now become open warfare. Julius Mosca seemed to be on the point of chucking out his guest, who was feeling in his pockets for his loaded revolver.

But suddenly Mosca relaxed, he became human again, and as he held out his arms to Scott a broad smile lit up his wicked face.

'Come, come, my dear Octopus,' he said. 'Forgive my impatience. Why should we quarrel about a few million pounds, and forged, at that? You haven't even heard my proposal.'

'Let me hear it, then,' growled Scott.

'It's a gigantic plan – bold, daring, magnificent, unique.'

These words seemed to arouse Octopus Scott's curiosity. A gleam of interest lit his eyes. He had a craving for real, not counterfeit, money which could never be satisfied. Also, the thought of leaving to Mosca alone the execution of such a tremendous scheme was too much for him, for he saw at once that, as sure as eggs are eggs, it would give this revolting enemy of his the opportunity of being the brain behind as much as 73 per cent of all international criminal activity.

'All right,' he said. 'Go ahead, I'm all ears.'

Julius Mosca puffed energetically at his cigar, then began: 'We'll have to act quickly. Speed is my watchword. Now if you. . . .'

And that was the end of the show. The screen was blank once more. Evidently Julius Mosca had stopped the camera by pressing a button on the electronic box which controlled it.

Everybody in the editorial office looked glum, everybody except Agaton Sax, whose face was as cheerful as ever.

'We'll have to do something about it,' Sergeant Antonsson shouted. He sounded angry as well as frightened.

'Damn it!' murmured Lispington, thoughtfully nibbling the tip of his left forefinger. 'What do you make of it, Agaton Sax?'

The master sleuth allowed himself a superior little smile.

'It all seems very simple,' he said, getting up from his chair.

'What do you mean, simple?' said Lispington impatiently.

'There are only two possible solutions,' said Agaton Sax casually. 'We have got to choose one or the other, or, of course, a combination of both.'

Lispington stared at him. He turned grey, then red, and finally crimson. He suppressed an oath as Agaton Sax sat down again, a cordial smile on his lips.

'Gentlemen,' he said, 'later I'll tell you what Mosca and Scott are up to. But for the present I am only going to make a few observations on the film we have just been watching. You notice Mosca didn't want to record that part of the conversation in which he outlined his great scheme to Octopus Scott. That would have been too great a risk to take. He only wished to demonstrate to Uncle Teetotum what a wonderful invention my photo-recorder is. After Octopus Scott had left, Mosca developed the film and sent the camera and the roll of film to Uncle Teetotum. As soon as Uncle Teetotum had seen them, he sent Lazy Bull with the camera and the film back to Mosca. Or rather, that's what he believed he did. As you all know, Lazy Bull made a perfectly natural mistake in giving the camera and the film to our friend Mr Nick.'

Two of those present heaved a deep sigh, and one of them, Mr MacSnuff, looked sadly at Agaton Sax, before saying:

'Is that all, Mr Sax?'

'Oh no. By no means. But it's all I can tell you at the moment. You must have confidence in me. I shall crush them.'

Agaton Sax was moved by his own determination. His eyes flashed angrily, and the others shrank back as if they would like to vanish through the wall. He paced up and down the room, hands behind his back, concentrating deeply.

'I've had enough of this! Why should you switch our speaking tube off, just because you're talking to those high-class fools up there?'

It was Aunt Matilda again. She was battering on the door, very angry indeed.

'You'd better tell those people who keep pestering me on the phone that I am *not* Swinging Susie nor am

I going to take over her part! Do you hear me, Agaton?'

Agaton Sax seemed dazed by this second interruption.

'What on earth are you talking about, Aunt?'

'About myself!'

'But you said something about Swinging Susie?'

'So I did, so I did.'

'But why?'

'Because *he* did.'

'He? Who's he?'

'The person who phoned me, of course.'

('That lady is extremely dangerous, always has been,' murmured Lispington to himself, slowly shaking his head.)

'Now tell me, Aunt, who phoned you about Swinging Susie? You know who she is, of course?'

'I know who she isn't. Me.'

'I know, Aunt. She's a vocalist.'

'I don't know what you're talking about, Agaton, but I know that three minutes ago there was a telephone call and a man with a silly voice said "Hullo, Miss, can you confirm that Swinging Susie has disappeared?" I asked him what on earth he was talking about, and he said, "I was asking you about Swinging Susie. Is it true that she's done a bunk? She is supposed to be singing at the Civic Banquet tonight, but she hasn't shown up yet." So I asked him why he thought the fate of this Swinging Susie person should be any concern of mine. He replied, "I thought that if Agaton Sax doesn't succeed in finding her, perhaps you could dress up as Swinging Susie and do her number for her at the Civic Banquet?"'

'I never heard such cheek in all my life!' said Agaton Sax.

'What am I to do now, Agaton?'

'Nothing, Aunt.'

'Nothing?' exploded Aunt Matilda behind the door. 'Well, I never!'

And off she went.

As Agaton Sax wiped his forehead, a slight twitch could be detected under his right eye. Quickly pulling himself together he said: 'Since you are not familiar with the complexities of the Swedish language, I'll explain what my Aunt has just been saying. You see, tonight the Town Council are the hosts at an important banquet, arranged to celebrate the inauguration of the Bykoping Skyscraper – a towering seventeen-storey building. In my capacity as chairman of the Festival Committee, I have the great honour of inviting you all to attend this banquet at 20.00 hours.'

'Hear! hear!' said the three English gentlemen enthusiastically, then, after a moment's pause, Inspector Lispington added more formally, 'How very kind of you, Mr Sax – but your Aunt?'

'My Aunt?'

'Well, she must have said . . . er . . . something else . . . she was . . . how shall I put it? . . . rather annoyed, or . . .?'

'Yes, well yes, she was,' said Agaton Sax somewhat flustered. 'You see, a well-known local vocalist, Swinging Susie, has been booked to sing at the Banquet, accompanied by the equally well-known group, the Soft Shoe Shufflers. It now seems that someone has phoned my Aunt and told her that Swinging Susie won't show up tonight . . .'

He fell silent, and for a few moments concentrated so hard on the problem Aunt Matilda had posed that he seemed quite unaware of his companions' presence in the room. There was something seriously worrying about Aunt Matilda's message, something that did not fit in at all with his ideas on this strange and important case, something that . . .

The others watched him in respectful silence. After a few minutes Inspector Lispington cleared his throat.

'Mr Sax,' he said.

No reply.

'Mr Sax, I . . .'

Still there was no reply. Agaton Sax seemed to be a thousand miles away – perhaps further.

'Mr Sax . . .'

Lispington still received no answer, but now a faint smile appeared on his lips, and he said in a loud voice:

'Sax Mr, little you a wouldn't Swinging Soft Susie tell Shoe more us about and Shufflers Banquet the and the?[1]

Agaton Sax shuddered as if he had heard the crack

[1]Scramble talk: (see *Agaton Sax and the Scotland Yard Mystery*) Mr Sax, wouldn't you tell us a little more about Swinging Susie and the Soft Shoe Shufflers and the Banquet?

of a whip too close to his right ear for comfort. Almost mechanically he answered: 'Mysterious what is this me worries phone about Swinging call Susie.[2]

Mr Nick and Mr MacSnuff looked at each other.

'Didn't I tell you Mr Lispington is a nut case?' Mr Nick's look seemed to say.

'And what about this Mr Sax – isn't he just as much of a nut case as Mr Lispington?' Mr MacSnuff appeared to reply.

Suddenly Agaton Sax drew himself up. He had come to an important decision.

'Gentlemen,' he said firmly, 'the Banquet will start at 20.00 hours as planned, that is, in four hours' time. I'll book rooms for you at the Metropolitan Hotel. A bit later on, Mr Lispington, I would like to have another word with you. I think what is required now is quick action.'

'You mean you think we should return to London immediately?'

'No, I don't think that would be the answer.'

'You mean, you think they are planning a coup somewhere else? In Lebanon? Bath? Khatmandhu or Lima?'

'Impossible to say.'

'For pity's sake, Mr Sax, say something!' Lispington exclaimed. 'You are keeping me in a state of unbearable suspense. Suppose they should strike at the very heart of Scotland Yard!'

'Quite possible. They're completely unscrupulous. You never know where they'll strike next.'

Lispington started to walk up and down the room, looking rather like a deeply disturbed elk.

'We must strike first,' he murmured, beating the palm of his left hand with his right fist.

[2]What worries me is this mysterious phone call about Swinging Susie.

'Right!' said Agaton Sax briskly. 'Would you care to return at 17.00 hours, Mr Lispington?'

As Agaton Sax's four guests took their leave, he crossed to the window and watched them emerge into the High Street. Lispington and Antonsson came first, then Mr Nick and Mr MacSnuff. The two policemen were chatting without much difficulty, obviously in English, for the Bykoping Police Force (Antonsson) had greatly improved its command of the English language in recent months.

Mr Nick and Mr MacSnuff, on the other hand, were walking in silence. They seemed to be avoiding each other's company as much as possible, though of course neither of them would have preferred to be with Lispington. It was as if they wished to demonstrate, by their mutual silence, that they did not really know each other at all, and that they cursed the very memory of that ill-fated day when they had met on a bench in Hyde Park.

Slowly, Agaton Sax pressed the editorial telescope to his right eye. He watched the 'doubles' with care. To an editor-in-chief and sleuth of Agaton Sax's calibre, no theory, no suggestion, however fantastic, could be dismissed. Any idea, however odd or unexpected, that came into his head had to be weighed in the balance, scrutinised, tested. For more than an hour now his brain had been exploring the possibilities of a fantastic notion. Now he must put it to the final test. *Was it possible that the doubles of Julius Mosca and Octopus Scott were in fact Julius Mosca and Octopus Scott, pretending to be their own doubles, Absalom Nick and Charlie MacSnuff?*

He lowered the editorial telescope. No. Now, he was absolutely sure of himself. The two 'doubles' were genuine, all right, they really were Nick and

MacSnuff. But this was perhaps the most worrying feature of all in the whole mysterious case.

Slowly he walked up to his desk and sank down in his editorial chair. He smoked pipe after pipe while going over, step by step, every aspect of this terrible mystery which, he felt sure, would shake both the Underworld and Interpol to their very foundations.

Suddenly, he picked up the telephone and dialled a number. He felt he must speak to his old friend, John Johnsson, Bykoping's chief brewer.

'Is that you, John? Agaton here.'

'Hallo, Agaton. Any crimes today?'

'Not yet. But there will be some.'

'What? You're joking, of course.'

'Perhaps. Let's hope so.'

'Not today, Agaton. Remember, this is the day of the Civic Banquet! You can't fly to Scotland Yard today.'

'Don't speak so loud, John, somebody might hear you. Now, listen carefully.' Agaton Sax lowered his voice. 'Can you still hear me? Good. It's the Banquet I'm calling you about.'

He sounded so full of foreboding that Johnsson was almost frightened.

'Nothing's gone wrong with the Banquet, has it?' he asked anxiously. 'You know how much we've all been looking forward to it.'

'Nothing's gone wrong yet, as far as I know,' said Agaton Sax. 'I'm phoning you about Swinging Susie.'

'Swinging Susie?'

'Yes!'

'Well?'

'Do you know her?'

'Me?' He laughed. 'No, Agaton, I don't.'

'But wasn't it you who booked her to come and . . .

sing at the Banquet? Singing is what it's called, isn't it?'

'I don't know much about it – singing, or droning, or crooning or whatever you call it. Swinging I think it is.'

'But where did you hear about her?' insisted Agaton Sax.

'Let me think. Yes, I remember. I rang up the *Musical Artists' Agency* and told them we wanted a good entertainer to follow the Mayor's Inaugural address, someone really funny. They said that they quite understood, we'd need cheering up after that. They gave me Swinging Susie's phone number, and I rang her up.'

'Where does she live?'

'In a village about forty miles from here.'

'And what about the Group?'

'It goes with her, so to speak. When you make a contract with Swinging Susie, it includes the Soft Shoe Shufflers.'

'Have they arrived yet?'

'I'm sure they have. The Banquet begins in a few hours, and I suppose they've got to rehearse and test the microphones and the loudspeakers, and so on. I know they're staying at the Metropolitan.'

'Thanks, John.'

Agaton Sax put down the receiver and rang the Metropolitan Hotel. Neither Swinging Susie nor the Soft Shoe Shufflers were there, but somebody had left a message with Reception to the effect that Susie and her Group would go on foot straight from the railway station to the Banquet.

Agaton Sax slowly stroked his immaculate moustache. Everything depended on his skill, courage, and ability to see more than the obvious. No one in the town had the slightest suspicion that at this

moment a colossal crime was in preparation – no one but he himself. Suppose things developed faster than he anticipated. Suppose the criminals. . . . Urgently, he shouted at the wall:

'We may be on to something really dangerous, Aunt! Come up at once.'

A minute later Aunt Matilda was standing in the editorial office, notebook and pencil in hand. Usually it was Aunt Matilda who made all important decisions and gave all the important orders in the house: she decided whether Agaton would have beef or lamb cutlets or pork spare ribs for lunch, how much light ale it was proper for him to drink, what vitamins he should take and at what hours, how thick his February underwear should be compared with that which he wore in May, what sort of socks could be allowed during the summer months, and so on.

But now and then, and particularly when danger

threatened, Agaton Sax, even in his own home, gave proof of an implacable stubbornness which made even Aunt Matilda shake. With a hand that trembled slightly she took down the orders Agaton Sax dictated.

'Good. Excellent,' he said cheerfully when at last he had finished. 'And now, my dear aunt, I trust that you will carry out my orders to the letter.'

At that moment, Lispington entered the room.

'Ah, here you are,' said Agaton Sax. 'Let's get to work straight away.'

In a few words he explained the whole situation to Lispington. Then he picked up the photo-recorder, and put it carefully into his briefcase.

'The curtain rises on our play, Lispington,' he said. '"All the world's a stage . . ."'

5

A disastrous banquet

It is not difficult to imagine the pride of Bykoping's citizens at the opening of its tallest building, its first 'skyscraper'. The celebrations were a big event in the history of the town.

As we have already said, there was to be a Civic Banquet. The Town Council had invited seventy-three leading citizens to be its guests, among them Aunt Matilda; but she had refused the invitation, with thanks, since it clashed with her 'knit-and-darn' evening, that is to say, the one evening a week she devoted to repairing Agaton's socks.

Right up to 15.00 hours Agaton Sax had been looking forward enormously to this, the year's big event. But by 19.45 hours as he walked across the road from his office to the skyscraper, he was too absorbed in complicated calculations to be looking forward to anything.

It was a fine, warm evening. One guest after another made his way to the skyscraper, and took the lift to the Festival Hall on the thirteenth floor.

I must look as cheerful as I can, Agaton Sax thought to himself. If the guests notice that I look anxious about the Banquet, some of them may begin to feel suspicious. Antonsson bothers me, he just might be tempted to start telling people what he knows.

Agaton Sax politely raised his black bowler hat to some of the other guests, accompanying his gesture with a benevolent smile. But inwardly he was burning with excitement.

He walked slowly into the large Festival Hall, allowing himself time to have a good look at all the other guests who were gathering there. Smilingly, he shook hands with the Mayor, the Chairman of the Town Council, the Vice-Chairman, the Chairman of the Revenue Board, and all the other chairmen and vice-chairmen of the various organisations in the town. He then strolled over to one of the windows, pretending to admire the splendid view of Bykoping. But actually he was on the look-out for something unexpected, for some clue, some detail, however small, that could be of value to him. Evidently, he thought, the gang's plans are very well laid. But they shan't find me unprepared either!

He went up to one of the head waiters.

'Has Swinging Susie arrived with the Group?' he asked, with a friendly smile.

'No, sir, but they are on their way. Though I must say they seem to be cutting it a bit fine, eh, sir? The people at the hotel tell us they are coming straight to the Banquet from the station.'

'I see.'

The guests' attention was caught by someone clapping his hands for silence. Everyone moved over to the banqueting table. Being one of the guests of honour, Agaton Sax had been placed at the Mayor's left hand. On the Mayor's right was Mr Lispington's place. Unfortunately it was empty. He had not turned up, and Sergeant Antonsson was also missing. Agaton Sax noticed this, not without certain misgivings. He nodded politely to Mr Nick and Mr MacSnuff, who had obtained permission to sit side by side so that they would not need to make conversation to strangers during the meal.

Three of the waiters had been sent to search the stairs and the lifts for Lispington and Antonsson, and even to shout their names in the basement, but there was no sign of either of them. The Mayor was irritated by the delay, because he was anxious to make his inaugural speech, which he had been hard at work on for the last few weeks. He decided he would wait no longer and launched into his beautiful oration, ending with the following words:

'And now, ladies and gentlemen, it is my pleasure to introduce the lovely Swinging Susie, accompanied by the Soft Shoe Shufflers. They have promised to entertain us while we eat. These charming young people tell me they are going to play for us some of Sweden's best-known and best-loved folk-songs.'

The moment the Mayor finished speaking, something remarkably like a violent explosion shook the door at the other end of the hall, and a deafening noise put an end to all conversation round the table, whether it had began already or was about to begin. Swinging Susie and her group appeared on the scene, brandishing their various instruments and resolutely storming the little platform. The Mayor, realising in a flash that his choice of entertainment had been a ghastly mistake, turned to Agaton Sax and said: 'My goodness, the modern generation are a bit . . . well, I thought . . .'

What he thought was drowned by the high-pitched wail of an unmuffled trumpet and a crashing of kettle-drums, while Swinging Susie, including the whole room in a sweeping gesture, roared at the top of her voice:

Yeppe-o, yeppe-o,
I love you so!

To anyone who knew anything at all about the art of pop music, it was quite evident that the six young men in Swinging Susie's group had not practised for more than half an hour at most. It was also open to doubt whether the trumpeter was aware that the trumpet is a wind instrument.

'This is a downright swindle,' roared the Town Clerk indignantly. 'I protested when I signed a contract of a hundred pounds for eight tunes – twelve pounds, ten shillings per tune – that it was far too much. But as we shan't be able to stand more than

one tune, they'll actually get a hundred pounds for just this one rotten song.'

The other guests, who knew nothing about the contract, cheered politely (though they were considerably frightened) when Swinging Susie and her group finished their first tune. The musicians were all dressed up as Mexicans or West Indians, and it was obvious, in spite of their friendly, innocent smiles, that they were determined, even if it meant a fight, to hold the stage until they had finished their act. However, Mr Johnsson, the brewer, was a match for them, and it didn't take him long to persuade them, forcibly, that it would be better for their health if they took a few minutes' rest.

Agaton Sax nodded, almost imperceptibly, to himself. All his forebodings were coming true. How lucky that he was well prepared for the fight!

As soon as he had seen Swinging Susie and her group come storming into the hall, he had known, with absolute certainty, that his calculations were correct. Within a few minutes he would be standing, or sitting, face to face with the two most dangerous criminals in the world, Julius Mosca and Octopus Scott! Unless . . .

The terrible truth was that Swinging Susie was not Swinging Susie at all, but the greatly feared Smiling Sandra Smith – a prima donna in the world of international crime, the opposite number, on the distaff side, of Julius Mosca or Octopus Scott.

This could mean only one thing: the bosses, male and female, of the underworld, had joined forces in a deadly enterprise – to crush Agaton Sax. It was this plan that Agaton Sax had anticipated and Julius Mosca had outlined to Octopus Scott at their meeting.

Smiling Sandra Smith had clearly gone to great pains to alter her appearance, since she was only too well known to the police, and her photograph could be studied in Scotland Yard's *Secret Code Register of Current Criminals*. But Agaton Sax, with uncanny perception, had guessed who the singer would turn out to be when he was told earlier that afternoon of Swinging Susie's sudden disappearance. Indeed, he could have told anyone who wanted to know the identity of all the Mexican or West Indian musicians in the group. He'd tangled with them all in his time – Laughing Willie Williams, Hopeless O'Donovan, Fat John, Dim Sven Gustaffson, Moscow Jim, Finn the Forger, and 'Cauliflower' Charlie.

But how had all these dangerous crooks managed

to invade the peaceful Festival Hall of Bykoping's new skyscraper? There was only one possible explanation: under the leadership of Mosca and Scott they had kidnapped Swinging Susie and her Soft Shoe Shufflers, locked them up somewhere, and then, using stolen instruments and clothes, invaded the Hall pretending to be a charming and harmless Swedish pop group.

At this crucial point, one question was of paramount importance: when and how would Julius Mosca and Octopus Scott enter the arena?

Agaton Sax got his answer much quicker than he had expected. The great double doors at the end of the Hall were flung open, and the two crooks came tumbling into the Hall with Lispington and Antonsson following hard on their heels, desperately snatching at a coat-tail or cuff in an effort to get hold of them, and shouting frantically, 'For the love of Mike, arrest them! Seize them! They are planning a desperate crime!'

But the two criminals had the unbelievable cheek to play the innocent. As they ran round the banqueting table at about 40 mph, they shouted furiously, at the top of their voices: 'For pity's sake, stop these madmen! Grab Lispington. How much longer are you going to allow this half-wit to terrorise innocent citizens all over Western Europe? Mr Mayor! Mr Vice-Mayor! Mr Chairman of the Town Council – Mr Vice-Chairman of the Town Council! Mr Sax! In the name of law and justice – stop Lispington and the Swedish madman!'

Three gentlemen and one lady fainted when they suddenly saw the two quiet Englishmen who had been at the Banquet since the beginning rushing round the table and at the same time sitting peacefully in their seats.

But Lispington and Antonsson were enraged and had no intention of giving up the chase. Having completed three laps of the table, the two runaways decided that it would be better to make a dash for it, and dodged out through the doors with Lispington and Antonsson on their heels.

Agaton Sax had half risen from his chair. He hesitated for a moment. Then he turned to the Mayor, excused himself, and hurried out. He saw the four men disappear down the stairs. Half a minute later he got the impression that the chase was over. It looked as if the policemen had caught up with their quarry. Or had they . . .?

He stood there, lost in thought. Down below, on the eleventh floor, he had spotted six men, silent, motionless. As Lispington and Antonsson leapt down the stairs in pursuit of the fugitives, the six men closed in behind them. They obviously intended to shadow the policemen and their prisoners.

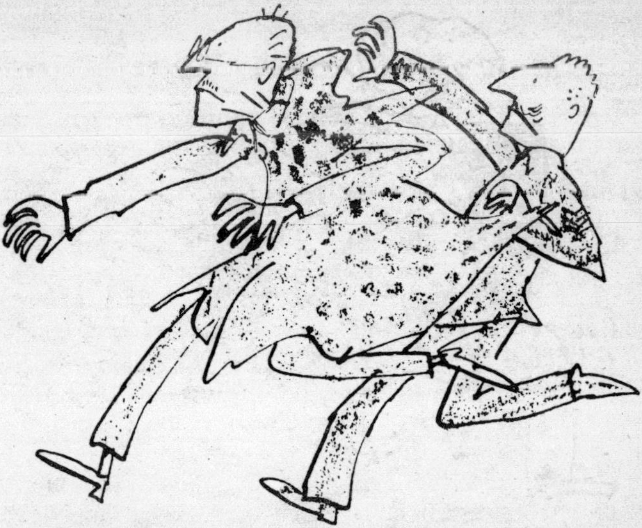

Agaton Sax went into action. He knew now what to do at this critical point in the drama. He returned to the Banquet Hall, walking with firm but lighthearted steps. He went up to Mr Nick and Mr MacSnuff, who were busy trying to explain to their neighbours what had happened.

'Gentlemen,' said Agaton Sax, beaming cordially, 'let me congratulate you! We've got Mosca and Scott at last. Your trials are over. Lispington and my plans have been one-hundred per cent successful – or even more. After the banquet I'd be glad if you'd both come and see me at home, so that I can tell you the whole story.'

He pressed their hands, and their faces were radiant as they looked first at each other and then at Agaton Sax. He returned to his seat, tapped his glass loudly and, when everyone had stopped talking, made the following short speech:

'Mr Mayor! Ladies and gentlemen! You have just

witnessed one of the most dramatic fights between the Law and the Criminal to take place in this century. This is an historic moment. There is no need to tell you that the Law has triumphed. Scotland Yard and the Bykoping Police Force, in the person of Sergeant Antonsson, have cooperated successfully in capturing two of the most prominent gang-leaders in the world, Julius Mosca and Octopus Scott, whom I myself had the honour of unmasking and bringing to court only a few years ago. Alas, only a short time later they escaped from prison. I beg you, ladies and gentlemen, to remember these two names, for by tomorrow they will be on the front pages of all the world's great newspapers, The London *Times*, the *New York Times*, the *Bykoping Post*. Here with us on this happy occasion, enjoying our splendid Banquet, are two honest English gentlemen, Mr Absalom Nick and Mr Charlie MacSnuff. As ill luck would have it, they happen to be as like Mosca and Scott as peas in a pod. In a little while I'm going to ask them to tell you all about their strange and disagreeable adventures, and I'll also reveal to you the nature of the secret plans which Inspector Lispington and I made that led up to this sensational capture. But before we do anything else, I would like to ask the charming Swinging Susie and her delightful Soft Shoe Shufflers to sing and play something soothing for us, so that we can resume our dinner in a mood of perfect happiness and tranquillity. May I also ask our deft and skilful waiters to set about the task of refilling our plates and recharging our glasses?'

An enormous cheer greeted this last request. Everyone toasted his neighbour, glasses clinked, and Mr Nick and Mr MacSnuff smiled and beamed upon each other and the company. Swinging Susie (alias Smiling Sandra Smith, remember) and her band of impostors struck up again, this time with their own rendering of that well-known, delightful old tune

Happa-dee-doo-dee
Gonna see you – ee

The terrible noise they produced put an end to the buzz of conversation that had broken out round the table, except for one remark that was clearly heard when, for some unknown reason, all the musicians happened to stop playing at the same moment:

'That caterwauling female must be Swinging Susie's mother!'

Agaton Sax missed nothing. The waiters were rushing here and there refilling plates and glasses. The dramatic events of the evening, and the amount of shouting they had had to do to make themselves heard, had had a stimulating effect on the appetites of the guests. They were all so busy eating, drinking and shouting, that none of them noticed Agaton Sax's quite extraordinary manners: with remarkable dexterity he was popping all his share of the food and drink into the sleeves of his jacket, where he had hidden two plastic bags (specially made to his own design) which closed automatically each time they received a fried potato, a parsnip, or a swallow of claret.

Was Agaton Sax really so mean as to smuggle home food and drink from the Civic Banquet? Of course not! There was a completely different reason for his antics.

When Swinging Susie (Smiling Sandra Smith) and her inexpert accompanists had struggled through to the end of their song, Agaton Sax tapped his glass again. At once there was a respectful silence. He rose from his chair and looked quietly round the Hall. He was about to deliver one of the most remarkable speeches in Swedish history.

'Mr Mayor – ladies and gentlemen,' he began solemnly. 'I'm sorry I have to interrupt your conversations, but there are a few words I'd like to say to you.'

'Long live Agaton Sax!' called out Bykoping United's former inside-right, Charlie Conk.

Agaton Sax raised his hand to ask for silence. As a veteran soccer referee, he was instantly obeyed by Charlie Conk.

'It is not every week we can celebrate the inauguration of a skyscraper in our town. I'm sure you will all agree with me that this is one of the most memorable days in our lives.'

Having pronounced these solemn and impressive words, he fastened his gaze upon the Mayor's wife, who was giving vent to such an enormous yawn that she seemed in danger of putting her jaw out of joint.

'I say, the Mayor's wife seems to be even more sleepy than I am,' whispered Johnsson, the brewer, stiffling a yawn himself.

'I assure you that my speech will not be long enough to send you to sleep,' Agaton Sax continued with a grim smile. 'What I would like to say is, that if, or rather, when, well, you see . . .'

He put his hand in front of his mouth in order to conceal his own yawn. At the same time, the Mayor waved pleasantly to his wife, and said: 'Sleep well, my love!'

(But he was too late, she was already fast asleep.)

Three seconds later, the Mayor himself leaned back in his chair, closed his eyes, and began to snore, only very softly, but he was certainly fast asleep.

Agaton Sax, who was rather pale, made an effort to pull himself together, but his eyes – normally so keen and penetrating – were glazed, and he didn't seem to be focusing properly.

'What I would like to say – as I said before – is that . . . That days most in lives of memorable one the is this our. Would thought have who – ten ago years only – spot Peterson's very on that where was Iron-mongers the conspicuously so situated, sky should scraper now magnificent a, later ten only years, beloved of Bykoping town our over tower? Witnessed progress have what we, what . . . ? What?'[1]

Under normal circumstances, an oration of this kind (delivered in elegant scramble talk) on such an occasion would have aroused considerable astonishment, or even provoked great anger among those present. But there were no such reactions. It seemed that this speech was so utterly boring – as distinct from most after-dinner speeches – that one guest after another, from the moment Agaton Sax had begun to speak, had fallen sound asleep.

Agaton Sax closed his eyes. Was he, too, talking in his sleep? He opened them again then resumed his oration, this time in scramble Graelic:[2]

'Holl-tyshen-gall, tall-hollen llan, phryl . . .'

Then he sank into his chair.

A few seconds later a harsh voice called out in English:

'He's asleep!'

It was Mr Nick. He and Mr MacSnuff had been watching Agaton Sax's face intently, and when the

[1] There is no need to translate Agaton Sax's scramble talk into plain English, but anyone who thinks it worthwhile is herewith authorised to do so.

[2] Agaton Sax is one of the 4,357 people in the world who have some knowledge of the very old and extremely difficult language, Graelic – an old Scottish dialect. Julius Mosca was a professor in Graelic Language and Literature. He devoted only his leisure hours to crime, but thanks to his supreme intelligence and total ruthlessness, he soon became one of the most dangerous men in the world. There was only one man who could crush him.

master sleuth suddenly passed from scramble English to scramble Graelic, a secret little smile flickered across Mr Nick's face, and he whispered to his colleague:

'Now we've got him. He's beginning to talk in his sleep.'

Grinning wickedly, Mr Nick and Mr MacSnuff leapt to their feet at precisely the same moment that Agaton Sax sank down in his chair.

'Smiling Sandra! Uncle Teetotum!' they called. 'The show is on!'

The awful truth now must be told. The two quiet gentlemen who had sat at the Banquet were not Mr Nick and Mr MacSnuff at all. On the contrary, they were Julius Mosca and Octopus Scott; while the two quiet gentlemen who had been so ignominiously chased round the table by Lispington and Antonsson an hour ago were the genuine Mr Nick and the genuine Mr MacSnuff.

A few other secrets can now be revealed. The six deft and skilful waiters were members of Mosca and Scott's gang in disguise. Among them were such leading crooks as 'Hairy' Herbert, Invisible Jackson, Ernest 'Fingers' Dodge, French Jules, the Sneaker, and Herr Gustaffson, an extremely dangerous man about whom we shall hear more later. They had sneaked into the restaurant kitchen, ambushed and locked up the staff, then dressed themselves in their clothes. After that, they had mixed a white powder in with the food and the wine.

This powder, though comparatively innocuous, was swift to take effect. Any of you who knows anything at all about drugs will not be surprised to hear that it was simply Hypnodiafragmasomniumperkominalmultidormatolinfermatolanparatexin.

6

An entanglement and a chase

An hour before Agaton Sax had set off for the Civic Banquet he had worked out for certain what was going to happen. He knew that Mosca and Scott would turn up with a number of accomplices, and that Swinging Susie and her band of impostors were in fact members of the gang in disguise. He was sure that Mosca and Scott's next move would be to put all the guests to sleep; then they could steal Agaton Sax's photo-recorder, kidnap Agaton Sax and Lispington, and demand a ransom of some two million (genuine) pounds for them.

The only event in the whole evening that had really surprised Agaton Sax was the dramatic dash round the banqueting table.

Before going on with the story it is necessary at this point to give an accurate account of what had been going on in Bykoping in the hours preceding the Banquet – that is, the very hours during which Agaton Sax and his English guests had been holding their conference in his editorial office.

A few days earlier, Mosca and Scott's secret agents had discovered that Mr Nick and Mr MacSnuff were going to Sweden. The two crooks realised immediately that their doubles could only be going there in order to visit their mortal enemy, Agaton Sax. They decided to strike back at once, and sent Mosca's second-in-command, Herr Gustaffson, in a private plane to Bykoping, with orders to have a good snoop round and prepare the way for a coup against Agaton Sax. Herr Gustaffson (not to be confused with Dim Sven Gustaffson, the well-known Swedish criminal) was a genuine Mexican from Chihuahua. He was called Herr Gustaffson, a Swedish name, because early in his career he had learnt Swedish, a very difficult language, which he could speak like a native. On his arrival in Bykoping he made it his business to find out all he could about the arrangements for the Civic Banquet; Swinging Susie's show, the number of guests, the menu, the names of the waiters, and so on.

In the afternoon of the following day, Mosca, Scott, and all their accomplices landed their two big helicopters on Johansson's meadow. From there they hurried to the Metropolitan Hotel, where they had already booked eight rooms.

As you will remember, Swinging Susie and the Soft Shoe Shufflers had arrived from another town some forty miles away. As soon as they got to the Hotel, Mosca and Scott introduced themselves to the singer, saying they were Hollywood impresarios who had travelled all the way to Sweden to listen to the famous Swinging Susie. Would she sing for them? Would she record something for them? Would she, moreover, like to sell three million records all over the civilised world. (Of course she would.) But hardly had she and her Soft Shoe Shufflers nodded their consent when the treacherous villains gagged and bound them, then carried them down to a room in the basement and locked them up.

Once this dastardly attack on seven honest musicians had been successfully completed, Mosca and Scott called a committee meeting. They met in Mosca's room on the third floor.

'My friends, loyal villains all, I hereby declare this meeting open!' said Mosca, banging the table with his revolver. 'First item on the agenda: Is anybody missing?'

'Yes, sir! I'm sorry to say that Invisible Jackson is missing, sir,' said Hopeless O'Donovan, who was responsible for seeing everyone got to meetings on time.

'Good! That's as it should be,' said Mosca.

'As it should be, sir?' queried Hopeless O'Donovan.

'Of course, you blockhead! He should be invisible, shouldn't he? Jackson! Come out! Show yourself.' Invisible Jackson, a swindler of unusual skill and dexterity, suddenly appeared. He had been hiding behind the heavy curtains.

Mosca again banged the table with his revolver.

'Smiling Sandra, will you tell us how far you have got with your plans? Have you and your six accomplices succeeded in forming a group?'

'Yes, sir, we have,' said Smiling Sandra Smith stepping forward.

'Have you been practising?'

'Yes, sir,' several voices called out enthusiastically.

'What instruments have you chosen?' asked Mosca suspiciously, and his tone sounded threatening.

'I play the fiddiolin, sir!' said Finn the Forger, formerly a printing press maintenance man, employed (rather unwisely) by the Dutch State Bank.

'The fiddiolin? You incompetent lout – do you mean the violin or the fiddle?' roared Mosca.

'I don't really know, sir, but my second cousin's brother had a . . . well, I suppose it was a fiddle, sir, and once I watched him playing, so I know exactly how to do it, sir.'

'All right. I suppose that will have to do. And you, Hopeless O'Donovan, what instrument do you fancy?'

'Me, sir? I think I'll deafen Agaton Sax with a *Saxophone*. That's a good one, isn't it, sir, ha ha ha!'

'Shut up!' shouted Mosca furiously. 'And you, "Cauliflower" Charlie, what is to be the victim of your efforts?'

'The floor-fiddle, sir!'

'And I'm blowing the concertina!'

'And I'm blowing the clarionetta!'

Julius Mosca, a man of immense knowledge and learning, reached boiling point as he listened to this recital of ignorance and musical incompetence by the luckless bunglers he had the misfortune to employ.

'Llah-ysh!' he growled through clenched teeth.

(This is Graelic and means: 'You useless nincompoops, can't you learn even the simplest words and phrases? I can't listen to you any longer! I give up!')

'Smiling Sandra.' He spoke in English again. 'Get this mob together and rehearse until 19.30. Do you understand? Good. Now listen carefully, all of you. Seven men, headed by "Hairy" Herbert, will present themselves at the Skyscraper Restaurant at 19.30, seize the kitchen staff, and dope them. Six others will watch all the entrances, exits and staircases. The Duke of Leicester Square will head this patrol. Smiling Sandra and her musicians will present themselves at the Restaurant as soon as "Hairy" Herbert and his gang have cleared the way for them. As for Octopus Scott and myself, we . . .'

He was interrupted by 'Cauliflower' Charlie, who was keeping watch by the window.

'Danger, sir! Lispington and the doubles are approaching the hotel.'

Mosca and Scott dashed to the window. Mosca rubbed his hands with glee, and a gleam appeared in Scott's eye.

'Superb!' murmured Mosca. 'Everything is working out just as I thought it would.'

In the street below, Mr Nick and Mr MacSnuff coldly took their leave of Mr Lispington, who then strolled off down the street. The two doubles entered the hotel.

Fifteen minutes later, they too were bound, gagged and locked in the basement. After another committee meeting in Mosca's room, the villains betook themselves to the Skyscraper Restaurant. They arrived in twos and threes, more than one of them with a beating heart, for they knew that Agaton Sax was a dangerous enemy. But Agaton Sax was nowhere to be seen. He wasn't in the street, he wasn't in the lift, he wasn't in the Restaurant.

We know already how well the crooks played their respective parts in the drama of the Civic Banquet: the strident musicians, the silent and efficient waiters, and Mosca and Scott themselves, who sat at the table, skilfully impersonating their own doubles. What we don't know is that just as the Banquet was about to start, strange things were going on in the High Street.

At 19.50 Mr Lispington entered the Police Station, for he had promised Antonsson to pick him up on his way to the Banquet.

While Antonsson was making a final readjustment to his tie, Lispington suddenly saw a fishing-line hanging from a hook on the wall.

'Why do you keep that line on the wall?' he asked curiously.

'Oh, that,' said Antonsson. 'Well, thereby hangs a tale, and a tangled tale, you might say.' He laughed at his little joke, and then embarked on an interesting and exciting story of a crime and the ensuing punishment that had to do with trout fishing. As

Lispington was a passionately keen angler, he insisted that Antonsson take down the line from the wall and show him exactly how the mysterious crime had been perpetrated and how Antonsson had managed to solve it.

As ill luck would have it, Antonsson succeeded in entangling Lispington in the long line, which, to make matters worse, was baited with thirty-seven hooks. He could not bring himself to destroy the line by cutting it, so he had to free his guest hook by hook, which took some time.

'By Jove!' Lispington exclaimed, looking at his watch as Antonsson freed him from the last hook. 'It's 20.15.'

As they hurried out into the High Street, they

heard the sound of running steps farther down the street.

Amazed, Lispington raised his right forefinger, and pointing at two men sprinting ahead of them, called out:

'Julius Mosca and Octopus Scott! This time they shan't get away!'

'Are you sure, Lispington! It might be their doubles!'

'No! That's impossible,' said Lispington firmly. 'We must arrest them at once. At last the hour has come. Forward, Antonsson!'

The two runners rushing down the High Street were, of course, Mr Nick and Mr MacSnuff. After two hours of frantic struggling they had at last managed to free themselves from their bonds just after 20.00 hours. Hungry and furious they had set off at once, anxious not to be late for the Banquet. It is easy to imagine their feelings when they caught sight of Lispington in the doorway of the Police Station. All their old fear of their energetic and relentless pursuer flared up, and in a desperate panic they made a dash for the safety of the skyscraper.

Naturally, Lispington and Antonsson mistook their flight for an admission of guilt, which accounts for the mad chase round the Banqueting table. But what happened after that? You may remember that Agaton Sax went to the top of the stairs, where he saw the four men disappear. He also saw six tough-looking thugs set off after the policemen and their quarry.

Lispington and Antonsson never caught up with Mr Nick and Mr MacSnuff, who hurled themselves into the High Street, where, after a moment's hesitation, they started to run towards the offices of the *Bykoping Post*, the only building in Bykoping, apart from the hotel and the skyscraper, that they

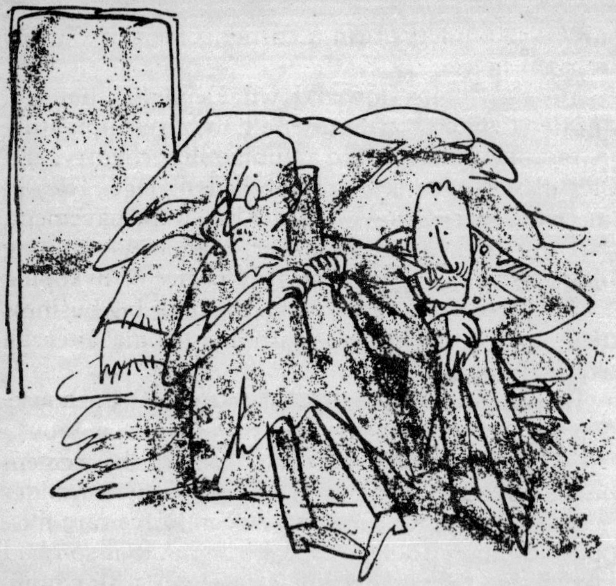

knew. Lispington and his Swedish colleague just caught a glimpse of their backs as they rushed through the main entrance.

'Come on, Antonsson!' panted Lispington, but Antonsson had turned pale, for he had heard, and seen, the six thugs pounding after them.

'We must hide, Lispington!' he whispered, and taking his friend's arm he ran along the pavement, round the first corner, round the second, and finally made for a big, half-finished building some fifty yards away. He knew that if they could only get to it with a good start, they stood a fair chance of being able to hide in the darkness of its shadowy walls.

The plan proved successful. They leapt up a flight of wooden stairs, squeezed through a narrow door, and crouched behind a pile of cement bags.

'Don't make a sound,' hissed Antonsson, as they

saw their pursuers turn a corner some thirty yards from the house.

The six villains slowed down. Evidently they had decided to tread warily; after all, they were operating in an unfamiliar town in an unfamiliar country, and they couldn't speak a word of the language. They lit fat cigars, paced slowly up and down the pavement, and put their heads together, obviously planning their next move with care. Any native of Bykoping seeing them would have taken them for big business men, managing directors strolling home after an excellent dinner.

The fact was they did not dare to enter the house. Nor did Lispington and Antonsson dare to come out.

Crouched in the darkness behind the cement bags, Lispington was slowly beginning to wonder whether he had perhaps made one of his rare mistakes. Suppose the two men he and Antonsson had just chased were really Mr Nick and Mr MacSnuff, innocent citizens, the victims of their unfortunate appearance?

He shivered with cold. After a little while his doubt became a certainty. There was really no reason to believe that Julius Mosca and Octopus Scott were in Bykoping at all. Why should they be? They were in London. (The reader must realise that neither Lispington nor Antonsson had noticed Mosca and Scott sitting at the table. They were going far too fast to notice any of the things that detectives normally notice when they are attending civic functions.)

'Antonsson,' he whispered; 'I . . .'

'Sshh!' said Antonsson, putting his finger to his lips.

Lispington obeyed. Antonsson was in command, this was *his* crime and *his* district. But Lispington had now made up his mind. The two men they had chased out of the skyscraper were Mr Nick and Mr MacSnuff. He felt greatly reassured. Within a few minutes he would . . .

But there we must leave him for the time being.

7

High tension

Having finished his after-dinner oration with a few words in scrambled Graelic, Agaton Sax sank into his chair. His head seemed too heavy for his neck as he slumped forward and rested his forehead on the white tablecloth. A hint of a snore was heard.

The crooks thought he was sleeping as heavily as the rest of the guests. They thought he had swallowed a few grammes of Hypnodiafragmasomniumperkominalmultidormatolinfermatolanparatexin with his fried potatoes and parsnips. They thought they had fooled him. The fools! They had watched him carefully during the banquet, and they thought that he had been eating and drinking just as heartily as all the others.

But they knew nothing of the hidden plastic bags. They knew nothing of his brainpower, either, it seemed. Seldom had Agaton Sax been more keenly awake. Seldom had he been called upon to play a more difficult part with more insight, imagination and intelligence. Not only did he deceive the villains, he also duped the Swedish guests, who noticed nothing, not even while they were still awake.

As his forehead was pressed against the very edge of the table, his mouth and chin jutted beyond it. He spoke very softly, saying in a clear whisper: 'Aunt Matilda! Calling Aunt Matilda! Put Plan 2B into operation. Repeat: put Plan 2B into operation. Everything is OK. I'll be with you soon. Remember: Plan 2B.'

No one in the Hall heard his whispered instructions, because the villains were all dancing like dervishes round the table, brandishing soup ladles, clarinets, wine bottles, violins, carving-knives, trumpets – anything they happened to be holding.

'We've vanquished Bykoping!'

'Fatso's caught, like ratso in a trap!'

'Two million quid! Genuine!'

'Long live Lispington!'

'Shut up!' yelled Mosca and Scott.

Agaton Sax whispered his message once again. He was wearing a mini-microphone in his tie, which was connected to a mini-transmitter in his fountain-pen. Aunt Matilda, equipped with a special receiver, was waiting for his call in the editorial office of the *Bykoping Post.* Immediately it came through she put Plan 2B into operation.

The crooks surrounded Agaton Sax. They carried him to the office of the Vice-Chairman of the Town Council, and put him down on a sofa. He appeared to be fast asleep. Julius Mosca and Octopus Scott laughed in triumph.

'Fantastic! Old Fatty walked right into the trap!' said Mosca. 'I swear by all that I hold sacred, that is all legal currency, that we'll make two million pounds out of this, and we've got old Fatty's camera into the bargain! Now for the newspaper office. Five men stand guard in the Banqueting Hall and the kitchen, three watch the exits, and two stay here to keep an eye on Agaton Sax. Now, where's my right-hand man?'

'Here,' said Uncle Teetotum quickly, looking up from the interesting task of taking a clarinet to pieces.

'Not you, stupid! I'm talking about Lispington. Where is he?'

This question caused some confusion, and there was a good deal of shouting, until two men were sent off to find Lispington.

'And now for the battle that will win the war,' said Julius Mosca, pointing a resolute finger in the direction of the building that housed the *Bykoping Post*. He

marched off, followed by Octopus Scott, Uncle Teetotum, Invisible Jackson, French Jules and Herr Gustaffson.

The offices looked peaceful in the warm summer dark. There was a light burning in Agaton Sax's own room on the first floor.

The crooks stopped. Mosca squeezed Scott's arm.

'Look!' he said. 'What's that?'

Octopus Scott stared coldly at a large poster fixed to the wall.

'What's that?' he asked. 'Do you mean that poster?'

'Yes, I do,' said Julius Mosca, who, being a professor of Graelic language and literature could usually hazard a guess when it came to reading a few words of other difficult and mysterious languages, such as Swedish. 'Herr Gustaffson,' he went on, 'you know Swedish – that's why we brought you here. Translate that poster into English.'

Herr Gustaffson put on his horn-rimmed spectacles, and translated for the benefit of the others:

LATE NIGHT EXTRA
STOP-PRESS

First with the news as always, the *Bykoping Post* is proud to report a significant event that took place this afternoon in the editor's office. At a short ceremony, the editor-in-chief, Agaton Sax, received from the hands of Chief Inspector Joshua H. Lispington of Scotland Yard, the sum of £15,000 (in gold sovereigns), a gift from the British Government to mark their respect and gratitude.

The story behind this quite exceptional generosity is that the money is the £15,000 found by the notorious gangster, Octopus Scott, while he was digging beneath his rhododendron beds. Agaton Sax caught Octopus Scott here in Bykoping a few years ago.

For the full story read tomorrow's paper!

Make sure of your copy by buying early.

Remember each edition of the *Bykoping Post* numbers only 814 copies.

Octopus Scott was by turns red with anger, white

with terror, and pink with pleasure. He was furious to learn that Scotland Yard had acquired his money, terrified lest it should by now have vanished into thin air, and overcome with relief when he realised that Agaton Sax could not possibly have spent much of it in just a few hours.

'Splendid!' he cried. 'I shall take back the money they stole from me. Justice will be done!'

'Just a minute, sir,' cautioned Mosca, who had listened with growing fury to Herr Gustaffson's translation of the poster. 'This could be a fraud – nothing but a pack of lies.'

'Are you calling me a liar, sir?' exploded Octopus Scott.

'No, not you. I'm referring to the poster.'

'What about the poster?' asked Octopus Scott.

'How do you know, Mr Scott, that the £15,000 that Agaton Sax got from Lispington today was your £15,000?'

'Because that's what the poster says,' said Octopus Scott.

'Poster, my foot!' said Mosca scornfully. 'All lies.'

'Are you accusing Scotland Yard of giving false information and spreading rumours?' exclaimed Octopus Scott. 'This is outrageous!'

'Remember, sir, that it's only a few years since Scotland Yard stole 23,400 Brosnian crowns, genuine ones not counterfeit, from me,' said Julius Mosca, whose eyes seemed ready to fill with tears at the recollection. 'And moreover,' he added, glaring threateningly at Octopus Scott, 'who is the boss here?'

The others murmured consent, and for the time being Octopus Scott had to stifle his impotent rage.

'Herr Gustaffson,' said Mosca, changing the subject. 'Lead on.'

Cautiously, they made their way into the building.

'Is this the door we want?' asked Mosca, pointing to a door with a large yellow notice pinned to it.

'No,' said Herr Gustaffson quickly. 'We mustn't go in there.'

'And why not, if I may be so bold as to ask?' snarled Octopus Scott, still in a temper.

'Because of the notice,' said Herr Gustaffson, and translated the inscription for them.

DANGER! HIGH TENSION CABLES
50,000 volts
No admission, not even on business – except for Agaton Sax and Aunt Matilda

Herr Gustaffson led the way past the door and up the narrow flight of stairs leading from the entrance hall to the first floor, where Agaton Sax's editorial office was situated.

Carrying revolvers in their right hands – Mosca had one in each hand – they cautiously pushed open the door and peered in.

The room was absolutely empty. The small white screen was still hanging on the wall, and, in full view on a flowerpot-stand in the middle of the room was Agaton Sax's miraculous invention, the photo-recorder.

'What luck,' said Mosca. 'Let's get the projector going straight away. It might tell us a few things we don't know.'

It took only a few seconds to get the projector to work. The film ran backwards at first, then jumped forward jerkily, but in a matter of minutes Mosca had it running smoothly.

And there he was on the screen! That odious little podge, that treacherous, unreliable, tale-bearing

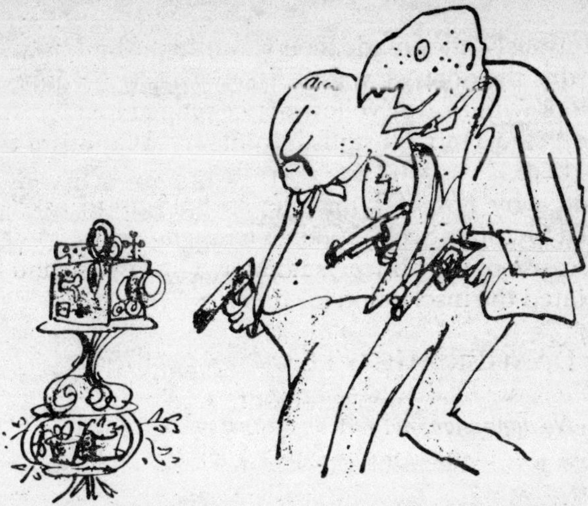

spy, Agaton Sax, number one hate of all right-minded criminals. He was sitting in his chair at his desk, his back to the camera. An elderly lady in a red-striped apron stood by his side. She was brandishing a large feather-duster in her right hand and she was clearly very angry.

The villains burst out laughing at this comic sight – not a very pleasant laugh, but they found the sight of Agaton Sax being threatened by an elderly lady very funny.

'There's going to be no playing the fool here,' said Aunt Matilda crossly. 'Haven't I made that clear once and for all?'

'But really, Aunt, there won't be any undesirables this time, I promise you, only a chap from Scotland Yard.'

'I don't care whether he comes from a Scottish Yard or an English Yard. I don't want him in my house!'

'But it's Lispington himself.'

'Lispington? I've never liked him since that time a few years ago when I had to pour two gallons of cold porridge over him – don't you remember, Agaton?'

'Of course I do, and so does he, I'm afraid,' said Agaton Sax. 'But this time Mr Lispington is bringing me some money, Aunt Matilda!'

'Money?'

'Yes, £15,000 in real gold sovereigns.'

'Why?'

'Because . . . oh, there he is now.'

The door opened, and Lispington entered followed by Sergeant Antonsson.

'Disgusting!' howled Uncle Teetotum as he saw Lispington appear on the screen.

'Revolting!'

'Horrible!'

'Turn it off.'

'We've had enough.'

'Shut up, you lousy layabouts! The successful criminal always respects his enemy.'

Lispington was carrying a gigantic briefcase in his right hand. As soon as he was inside the room he addressed himself to Agaton Sax and made a long and solemn speech. Then he opened the briefcase which he had put down on the floor beside his right foot. Agaton Sax peered into it and blushed with pleasure. (It was a colour film.)

'Thank you, Mr Lispington,' he said. 'This is indeed a pleasant surprise. The money will come in handy next week because I plan to come to London and help you to find and arrest Mosca and Scott. Since I took this money from Octopus Scott after I had run him down here in Bykoping, I feel entitled to use it in order to recapture him.'

'What an excellent idea,' said Lispington approvingly.

'The traitor!' hissed Julius Mosca between his teeth, but it was impossible to decide whether he meant Lispington or Octopus Scott.

'Have you got a strong-room, Mr Sax?' Lispington asked.

'Of course – I have a spacious strong-room, 7 foot 4 inches by 5 foot 3 inches, in which I keep all my criminal equipment – or perhaps I should say all my equipment for detecting crimes – registers, clues, exhibits, fingerprints, and so on. Let's deposit the briefcase in the strong-room.'

Agaton Sax and Lispington went into the strong-room through a door beside a big bookshelf. And that was all. The screen went blank.

Mosca and Scott made a dash for the strong-room door.

'The boss first, and I'm the boss!' shouted Mosca, pushing Scott out of his way and squeezing through the door before he had had time to open it properly.

At the far end of a short, dark passage there was a heavy steel door with a complicated combination lock.

'Herr Gustaffson,' roared Mosca, 'open this door!'

Uncle Teetotum switched on his electric torch. Herr Gustaffson, a mathematical and mechanical genius, put on a pair of steel-rimmed spectacles and fiddled with the lock. Three minutes later he had the door open.

Mosca and Scott tumbled into the strong-room, which closely resembled a library, with books, files, boxes and other exciting objects neatly arranged on the shelves along the walls.

In the middle of the floor stood the briefcase.

With a grunt of triumph Mosca threw himself on it. He flung it open with a vicious tug.

The other villains, who had hesitated at the door,

were slowly trickling into the room. Only Herr Gustaffson stayed in the editorial office, cautiously keeping an ear open for suspicious sounds.

Julius Mosca, the dreaded gang-leader, was actually trembling in a fever of greedy excitement as his eyes searched the inside of the briefcase.

It was empty.

What a dreadful sight. The crooks stood motionless, as if paralysed by a powerful electric shock. Then they all began to shiver – even the really tough and callous ones like Uncle Teetotum and Octopus Scott.

But before Julius Mosca's wrath had time to burst forth in the violent explosion they all feared, something utterly unexpected happened. Moved silently, as by an invisible hand (could Agaton Sax have been responsible?) the massive steel door of the strongroom clanged shut with a tremendous bang. Mosca, Scott and three of their leading accomplices were caught like rats in a trap.

Agaton Sax's superior intelligence had triumphed.

Only Herr Gustaffson had escaped. After a quick glance round the room he bolted down the stairs.

Behind the door marked DANGER! HIGH TENSION CABLES! Aunt Matilda was sitting in a comfortable yellow rocking-chair. She was, as usual, knitting. This was in fact her 'knit-and-darn' room – a pleasant retreat which she had furnished with, among other things, an old radio set and some twenty pot plants. But there was something else besides Aunt Matilda's belongings in the little room. In one corner stood a closed-circuit television set. In Agaton Sax's editorial office a television camera and a microphone were hidden behind a large picture on the wall. The camera and the microphone transmitted pictures and sound to Aunt Matilda's television set. This arrangement meant that Aunt

Matilda could watch and listen to all that the villains did and said in the editorial office. After they had dashed into the strong-room, it was she who pressed the button that closed the heavy door, trapping everyone except Herr Gustaffson.

'Oh gracious!' said Aunt Matilda as she saw that one of the villains had escaped and disappeared down the stairs. 'What a pity I can't tell Agaton until he calls me,' she thought, looking at a small microphone that stood on the table beside a loudspeaker.

At that moment, a low, clear voice was heard from the loudspeaker.

'Aunt Matilda? Over.'

'Agaton! Are you all right? Over!'

'Yes! Over.'

'Where are you?'

'The Banquet is over. Over.'

'Are you awake? Over.'

'Am I awake? Yes. But everyone else is asleep. Over.'

'Where are you, Agaton? Over.'

'I'm in the office of the Vice-Chairman of the Town Council. Can I have your report, please. Over.'

'First part of Plan 2B successfully carried out,' said Aunt Matilda briskly. 'I took the poster you gave me and stuck it on the wall. Over.'

'Good. And what about the second part of Plan 2B? Over.'

'Also successfully carried out. I put the empty briefcase on the floor of the strong-room, and rigged the folio-decoder in the . . .'

'I apologise for interrupting, Aunt, but it's called the *photo-recorder*. Over.'

'It doesn't matter what it's called, Agaton, as long as I rigged it all right. Over.'

'Agreed. Then? Over.'

'Then I saw the two Englishmen coming – the same ones who were here earlier this afternoon and who . . .'

'They were *not* the same Englishmen, Aunt,' said Agaton Sax. 'They were their doubles. Over.'

'I see what I see, Agaton! I don't know about any doubles, as you call them. How could they be double if there were only two of them? In that case, there should have been four, shouldn't there? Over.'

'It doesn't matter, Aunt. Over.'

'Well, you know who they were, Agaton. One was Mr MacSniff and the other was Mr Nuck. And then there were four others who . . .'

'I must apologise for interrupting again, Aunt, but you haven't got their names quite right. Still, never mind. What happened next? Over.'

'They watched the film you made this afternoon with that dreadful Mr Nispington, or whatever he's called; and when they had seen it, they all rushed to the door of the strong-room – just as you had planned it, Agaton. I pressed the button, the door closed with a bang, and they were trapped. Over.'

'Bravo! Aunt. Did you get the lot? Over.'

'No, Agaton, I'm sorry. One of them escaped. He sneaked down the stairs, and disappeared. Over.'

'Who was it? Over.'

'Who? I don't know for sure. But it wasn't one of those who came here earlier this afternoon. Over.'

'Good. I'll come as soon as I can. Over.'

'What shall I do now, Agaton? Over.'

'Nothing. Over.'

'But I can hear something.'

'What sort of something?'

'Voices.'

'Whose voices?'

'I don't know.'

'It couldn't be the villains, could it, escaped from the strong-room?'

'Now, that's a very stupid thing to say, Agaton. You know very well that they can't get out of that room! Wait a minute, I think I've got it. It must be some people walking up the High Street.'

'Be careful, Aunt!'

'I am careful. Yes, they're coming nearer. They are English voices. O yes, now I can hear. It's that intolerable man from London!'

'Do you mean Lispington?'

'Yes, the one I covered in cold porridge.'

'Good Heavens!' said Agaton Sax. 'Now you must really promise to take care.'

'He's going upstairs. He's got somebody with him. It must be Antonsson.'

'Antonsson and Lispington together! Great Scott! Now we are in an extremely dangerous position, Aunt Matilda. Heaven only knows what these two can cook up when they get together.'

'What shall I do, Agaton?'

'You must . . . Wait a minute . . . You . . . I . . .'

Suddenly Aunt Matilda's loudspeaker went dead. Communication between her and Agaton Sax, a prisoner in the skyscraper, was broken.

8

Aunt Matilda stands guard

Hearing nothing more from her nephew, Aunt Matilda picked up her knitting again. She was quite calm and composed, and not the least afraid of the villains, for the simple reason that she did not believe in them, any more than she believed in ghosts. She never had. But she did not like the two tall policemen.

It was, as she had told Agaton Sax, Antonsson and Lispington who were now hurrying up the stairs. You will remember that they had spent a long time hiding behind a pile of cement bags, waiting until they could be quite sure that their pursuers had returned to the skyscraper. Then they slipped into the street again, and hurried off to the office of the *Bykoping Post.*

You will remember also that Lispington had reached an important conclusion while he was crouched behind the cement bags. He had decided that the two men he and Antonsson had chased so energetically round the Banqueting Hall were in fact Mr Nick and Mr MacSnuff. Now he was anxious to make amends for his mistake.

Aunt Matilda hesitated for a moment as she heard the two policemen pass her door on their way to the stairs. Should she . . .? Yes, she thought she'd better . . . She opened the door.

'Antonsson!' she called out.

The two men stopped dead at the foot of the stairs.

'Yes?'

'It is I!' said Aunt Matilda dramatically, brandishing a knitting-needle.

'What on earth are you doing, Aunt Matilda?' said Antonsson, perplexed.

'Knitting, of course.'

'Knitting? Why?'

'Because Agaton needs a new pair of socks.'

'Can't you buy him some new ones at the men's outfitters?'

'No, they get more expensive every time I go there.'

'But I bought a pair yesterday, and they were only three-pence more than the ones I bought last year.'

'Yes, but they've done away with the rebate they used to offer, so in fact you're paying sevenpence a pair more now.'

'No, no, you've got it all wrong. The rebate was only two per cent, and it was never automatic, you had to spend more than £70 per year in order to get it, which would mean at least ninety pairs of best-quality socks.'

'In the name of goodness what on earth are you arguing about?' called out Lispington, who was getting more and more impatient. 'I'd better warn you about this woman, Antonsson – she's a dark horse, you never know what she's going to do next.'

'What do you want, Antonsson?' demanded Aunt Matilda. 'And why have you brought that pest here?'

'Well, we were wondering if you'd seen the two Englishmen who called on Agaton Sax earlier today.'

'Nuff and MacSnick, you mean?'

'That's right.'

'You've nothing to worry about, they're safely under lock and key.'

'Under lock and key? What on earth do you mean?'

'What did she say?' asked Lispington.

'I said they're safely under lock and key.'

'She said that they're safely under lock and key.'

'Under lock and key? Why?' cried Lispington in despair.

'Why are they under lock and key?' asked Antonsson.

'Because Agaton said so, of course.'

'But why?'

'Why? Because he thought they were villains, but they're not. I can tell you that.'

'Of course they're not, *I* can tell you that!' said Antonsson in a superior tone, since it was his job to know who was innocent in Bykoping and who wasn't.

'There's no time to lose,' said Lispington wretchedly. 'What a disaster! Scotland Yard will get the blame for this as usual. Mr Nick and Mr MacSnuff are bound to write to the Lord Chancellor, lodging another complaint against me. How rotten! Let's free them now and apologise, that might help a bit.'

He ran up the stairs two at a time, and rushed into Agaton Sax's editorial office.

'Where are they?' he asked, looking round frantically.

'In there,' said Antonsson, panting in behind him and pointing to the strong-room door.

'Where's my special all-purpose combination lock skeleton key?' exclaimed Lispington, fumbling in his pocket and bringing out a strange-looking device which he applied to the lock.

Not a sound could be heard from behind the steel door. The silence seemed ominous to Lispington.

'Hallo! Mr Nick! Mr MacSnuff!' Are you there?'

There was a noise like a grunt.

'It's all right, I can hear you. You'll soon be free,' said Lispington, soothingly. 'I'm sorry to say there has been an unfortunate mistake. Most regrettable . . . I do apologise . . . It won't happen again . . . I'm just working on the lock now. A thousand apologies, Mr Nick and Mr MacSnuff; you see, it was that impetuous lady who locked you up . . . it wasn't my fault, really, I knew nothing about it until two minutes ago. You can count upon the usual compensation even though Scotland Yard is not actually involved. She's impossible, you know, sticks at nothing . . . very regrettable . . . That's it, nearly done . . . Are you still there?'

Another grunt was heard. Lispington worked all the harder.

'I've almost finished. Keep your spirits up! Of course you're pretty used to being safely housed, so to speak, aren't you? Forgive my little joke. You'll get compensation even though you weren't apprehended on Her Majesty's soil.'

Click! The door swung open. With a cordial smile Lispington held out his hand to the man he believed to be Mr Nick, but who was in fact Julius Mosca.

'Please forgive me, Mr Nick,' he said, warmly shaking Mosca's hand.

'Of course! You're welcome!' roared Mosca in a foaming fury. Violently he pulled Lispington into the strong-room. At the same time the other villains flung themselves upon Antonsson, and three minutes later the two wretched men were bound hand and foot and tied to two chairs. At last Lispington realised his mistake. He had been right in thinking that it was Mr Nick and Mr MacSnuff he had chased round the table, right in believing that it was those two he had

seen rushing down the street towards the office of the *Bykoping Post*. Where he'd gone wrong was in not realising that they had taken shelter in the basement, where they were still sitting, quietly playing backgammon and waiting for Lispington to arrest them or Agaton Sax to set them free.

Mosca brushed the dust off his hands then glanced spitefully at Lispington.

'Now, most honourable cop, we are going to take you and that revolting little fat friend of yours back to London, where the British Government, or Scotland Yard, or the Bank of England, or Interpol, or whoever feels like it, can have the honour of handing over a ransom of £2,000,000. Real money, no forgeries, mind.'

At this point he shouted to his assistants one after the other in quick succession, and they jumped to obey as if he had taken a whip to them.

But, just as Mosca and Scott were leaving the editorial office, the telephone on Agaton Sax's desk rang shrilly.

We must now go back to Agaton Sax, whom we last heard of seven minutes earlier, when he spoke to Aunt Matilda in her knitting room. What had been happening to him while the villains were invading his office and being locked up by Aunt Matilda?

You remember that when the villains thought he had fallen asleep at the Banquet they carried him to the office of the Vice-President of the Town Council, and two of them were ordered to stay and watch him. Although he pretended to be fast asleep, his name was so feared in the world of international crime that the villains didn't relax, they considered that he might be extremely dangerous and unreliable even in his sleep. How right they were – especially as he was not asleep at all!

One of them, a nephew of the notorious Little Brother, posted himself at the door. The other, Hopeless O'Donovan, sat down on a chair with his back to one of the walls. Not for one second did they take their eyes off their prisoner. Agaton Sax had been placed on a comfortable sofa. The villains were quite happy, knowing that Mosca and Scott and most of the other members of the gang would be back soon. How consoling it was for them to know that their ordeal – being alone with Agaton Sax – would not last for more than twenty or at the most thirty minutes!

Even so, it was a strain, and Little Brother's nephew nervously shifted his weight from one foot to another. Hopeless O'Donovan, who was sitting down, crossed and recrossed his legs. He looked at his watch.

'What's the time?' he asked Little Brother's nephew.

'Four minutes later than when you last asked.'

'Why haven't they come back yet?'

'Calm down, fusspot.'

Little Brother's nephew drummed with his fingers on the wooden doorframe. Then he lit a cigarette.

Hopeless O'Donovan sniffed.

'What are you smoking?' he asked.

'*London Bridge*,' said Little Brother's nephew. 'Why?'

'Because there's a smell of burnt varnish in this room.'

'Burnt varnish? What are you talking about? Have you ever heard of an Englishman smoking burnt varnish?' retorted Little Brother's nephew angrily.

'I didn't say I had, I said there's a smell of burnt varnish in this room. Why?'

And he sniffed again, several times.

'I don't like it!' he exclaimed. 'Put that cigarette out, they're a damned rotten brand anyway. Put it out!'

'Why should I?'

'Because there must be something else burning in this room.'

'Burning?'

'Can't you smell it?'

Little Brother's nephew turned pale. He stubbed out his cigarette and sniffed the air.

'There!' shouted Hopeless O'Donovan, pointing. He leapt out of his chair and ran across the room.

In the opposite corner a little puff of smoke suddenly became an enveloping cloud.

'Help! Get the police! Call the fire-brigade!' shouted Little Brother's nephew, flapping his arms helplessly.

'Unlock the door, we've got to get out of here,' roared Hopeless O'Donovan, dashing for the door. But Little Brother's nephew had had exactly the same idea, so they crashed into each other with a jolt that knocked them silly. Meanwhile, the smoke had become so dense that it formed a thick, protective bank of mist between them and Agaton Sax.

'I can't see an inch in front of me, let alone a foot,' shouted Hopeless O'Donovan, desperately tugging at the door-handle, while his colleague made frantic efforts to undo the lock.

At last they got the door open and tumbled out of the room, coughing, and with their eyes smarting from the heavy smoke.

Behind the smoke curtain Agaton Sax smiled happily. He was wearing a gas mask which he kept specially in one of his pockets for this kind of emergency. It was he who, unobserved by the villains, had flung a miniature smoke bomb into a corner of the room as they were carrying him to the sofa. The bomb was practically invisible, hardly bigger than a pea or a coffee-bean. He had set its clock so that it was timed to go off three and a half minutes after being thrown on the floor.

The whole room was now filled with smoke, and Agaton Sax could hear the two crooks on the other side of the door trying to decide what to do with the fat little Swede on the other side of the smoke screen. He jumped up and groped his way to the door at the other end of the room. It was unlocked. Opening it cautiously, he peeped out.

The corridor was empty. Agaton Sax made a dive for the room next door, which turned out to be a small committee room. The first thing he did was to switch on his mini-microphone and call up Aunt Matilda. It was this conversation you listened in on earlier.

When Aunt Matilda told him that Lispington and Antonsson were entering the office of the *Bykoping Post*, Agaton Sax felt a shiver of fear. This, he thought, was probably far more alarming than anything that had happened since the gang's arrival in Bykoping. He had a sudden terrifying vision of two tall, stooping men walking up the stairs with grim, stern faces. . . .

'Aunt!' he said. 'You must . . . Just a minute!'

He heard a noise in the corridor, and knew he must keep absolutely quiet. Unfortunately, at that moment he made one of his rare mistakes, he forgot to switch off the little receiver that brought Aunt Matilda's voice to him. It was built into his watch, and as he stood there, listening with bated breath to the steps in the corridor, he suddenly heard Aunt Matilda's clear, incisive voice:

'I'd better boil up some more porridge, Agaton.'

Agaton Sax silenced her by pressing a minute button on the watch.

But it was too late. It was Little Brother's nephew outside the corridor and he had evidently heard something that aroused his suspicion.

'Who's in there?' he said.

'It's me!'

'Who?'

'"Cauliflower" Charlie,' said Agaton Sax, in perfect imitation of his hoarse, distinctive voice.

'Oh, it's you, Charlie! What are you doing there? I thought you went with the Bosses.'

'No, I didn't,' said Agaton Sax. 'You see, I was just about to follow the others when I saw that fat little man, Ag- or At-something, Atom Sax, come staggering out of that room full of smoke. So I grabbed him.'

'You did, Charlie! That's great!'

'Won't you join me, Little Brother's nephew?' said Agaton Sax with a cunning smile. He took up his position just beside the door.

'I'm just coming, and Hopeless O'Donovan is with me,' said Little Brother's nephew. Five seconds later the door opened and the two villains entered the room, quite unaware of the danger looming behind the door. With one swift movement Agaton Sax pulled them into the room, and dashed out himself. He slammed the door and locked it from the outside.

'You dirty traitor, we'll report you to the Boss for this!' they shouted furiously, banging on the door.

In vain. Agaton Sax slipped into another room and took a little walkie-talkie out of one of his pockets.

'Hallo, hallo, Aunt Matilda, are you there?'

'Of course I am.'

'Good. What has happened?'

'I've dropped two stitches. How can you expect me to knit with this terrible noise going on all the time?' she continued angrily. 'Who are they, Agaton?'

'Who are you referring to, Aunt?'

'To all these people who keep running in and out, up and down the stairs, in and out of your room. Sniff and Snuff and Snack, or whatever they're called, and that terribly annoying Englishman, and Antonsson, and . . .'

'Well you see, Aunt Matilda, this is . . .'

'. . . and what's more they're all foreigners, and they keep jabbering and chattering and tittle-tattling away. There's one they call Herr Gustaffson, and then . . .'

'Herr Gustaffson? I warn you, Aunt Matilda! He's not just dangerous, he's . . .'

'It doesn't matter what he is, because he's gone.'

'Gone? What do you mean? Isn't he locked up with all the others?'

'No, he just walked out.'

'Walked out? Well, what about Antonsson and Lispington?'

'They're here all right.'

'Where?'

'They've just gone upstairs.'

'What for?'

'I don't know, Agaton, how can I when I'm trying to knit – and how can I knit when they won't leave me in peace?'

'Aunt, for heaven's sake look at the television screen. Can you see Lispington and Antonsson in my room? Are they still there?'

'Oh yes. I can see them now. They are just trying to open the door of the strong-room.'

'Good heavens!' exclaimed Agaton Sax, caught off guard. 'This is disastrous! Try to stop them, Aunt.'

'How can I – I would get in a mess with my knitting and drop a lot of stitches if I tried to stop them. Besides you know they'll stick at nothing – not those two.'

'But what are they doing, Aunt?'

'At the moment they are setting free Mr Snick and Mr MacStuck. And now . . . What on earth's happening?'

'Go on, tell me. What is it?'

'Now they're taking them prisoners. They're flinging themselves furiously on to them, they're tying them up.'

'Who's tying who up? Who is who? Who's doing what?'

'Stick and MacSnack are tying up Antonsson and that tall insufferable Englishman. They oughtn't to do that, ought they? Now they are locking them up in the strong-room.'

'Don't move, Aunt Matilda! You are in an extremely dangerous position. But everything will be OK. Just keep on telling me, all the time, what they are doing.'

While Aunt Matilda was telling him of these dramatic events, which were even now coming to a head, Agaton Sax's brain was working with its usual phenomenal speed and clarity. Suddenly he knew what his next move must be.

He picked up the phone and dialled the number of the *Bykoping Post*.

'The telephone is ringing in your room,' said Aunt Matilda.

'I know,' said Agaton Sax, 'I'm ringing my own number. I'll switch off the walkie-talkie now, but stand by, Aunt, I'll contact you again.'

9

The elevation of Herr Gustaffson

The telephone bell cut through the quiet of the editorial office like a sharp knife. The villains stood, fixed to the spot, gazing in horror at it. It rang again. Mosca looked at Scott, who looked back at Mosca.

'I'll take it,' said Octopus Scott.

'No, it's for me,' said Mosca, coldly superior. He picked up the receiver. 'Hallo.'

'Hallo,' said Agaton Sax in Herr Gustaffson's easily recognisable voice.

'Who is it?' said Mosca, suspiciously.

'Herr Gustaffson, of course. Thank Heavens I've got you. It is Julius Mosca, the Boss, I'm speaking to, isn't it?'

'Of course.'

'Who is it?' whispered Octopus Scott. 'Don't let him take you in – he may be an imposter.'

'It's all right, I recognise his voice,' answered Mosca, covering the mouthpiece with his hand. 'Hallo, Herr Gustaffson, are you still there? Good. What became of you? You were with the rest of us when we were locked up, weren't you?'

'I was lucky. I happened to be standing just outside the door of the strong-room when the door swung shut. Are you free again?'

'Yes. But where are you, Herr Gustaffson?'

'I'm in the skyscraper. But I'm afraid I've got bad

news for you. That's why I'm ringing, actually. I want to warn you that . . .'

'What are you trying to tell me?' exclaimed Mosca, turning pale. 'Do you mean that Agaton Sax has escaped?'

'Help! Help!' several of the villains dashed for the door in a wild panic.

'Stay where you are, you dirty cowards! Herr Gustaffson – are you there? Of course I wasn't referring to you. What were you saying?'

'You asked me whether Agaton Sax had escaped. Well, he hasn't, thank heavens, that would have been disastrous,' said Agaton Sax, still in Herr Gustaffson's voice. 'No, it's something quite different.'

'What is it?'

'Treason!'

'Treason! How horrible!'

'I caught the traitor in the act.'

'Did you indeed, Herr Gustaffson?' Mosca was trembling with rage. 'Tell me all about it.'

'Certainly, Mr Mosca. You see, when I realised that I couldn't possibly get you out of the strong-room alone, I dashed over to the skyscraper. I decided to make a quick inspection of the building – and can you imagine what I found in the basement? No, Mr Mosca, you can't. Not even in the worst of nightmares could you imagine anything so dreadful.'

'Tell me.' Mosca was dancing about in an agony of suspense.

'In one of the cellars I found Smiling Sandra Smith. And can you guess what she was doing? She was sitting there, in semi-darkness, and she was counting . . .'

'Counting what?'

'Money.'

'Money?'

'Yes.'

'Ah!'

'She was counting the £15,000 sterling which belong to you, Mr Mosca!'

'Ah! How bitter! Such treachery! Revolting!'

'She didn't see me, absorbed as she was by her own greed, and I sneaked out again. Now, as you know, Mr Mosca, Smiling Sandra Smith is one of Octopus Scott's gang, and she considers the £15,000 to be his. When Octopus Scott discovered that Lispington intended to present Agaton Sax with the money, he was determined to get it for himself, so he ordered Smiling Sandra Smith to slip in to the *Bykoping Post* before *we* got there. She stole the money from the briefcase. Do you follow me?'

Julius Mosca, weak with fury, had to grip the edge of the table to prevent himself from collapsing on the floor.

'Black treason! Appalling villainy! Has he no

moral sense? Is there no honour left among thieves?' he moaned softly. Aloud he said:

'I understand.'

'I'm on your side, Mr Mosca, you can depend on me.'

'Good. I'm glad of that.'

'But I demand £5,000 sterling.'

'What?'

'Five grand – in Bank of England notes.'

'I don't think I heard you correctly, Herr Gustaffson! Will you repeat that?'

'You heard me, Mr Mosca. Take it easy. Either give me five grand, or I'll beat it with the whole fifteen! Remember, Mr Mosca, I hold the trump card. I can take that money off Smiling Sandra Smith right now, on the spot, and say goodbye to you. But I don't do that, because I'm an honest man. I've never appreciated Mr Octopus Scott's strong-arm methods, you see. No, I'll only keep five grand, you can have the rest. Then we hand Mr Scott over to Scotland Yard.'

'I agree. Now what do we do?' said Mosca, puffing excitedly at his cigar, and forgetting everything but the prospect of getting hold of his money.

'Listen carefully, Mr Mosca.'

'What are you two blabbing about?' shouted Octopus Scott, who was beginning to feel suspicious.

'Shut up!' ordered Mosca peremptorily. 'Herr Gustaffson has some extremely important news.'

'Hallo!' said Agaton Sax. 'Are you still there, Mr Mosca?'

'Yes, I'm listening.'

'Good.' (Agaton Sax lowered his voice to a whisper.) 'Tell Octopus Scott and the others that the money is hidden in a secret drawer at the far end of the strong-room. When they've all rushed in there to look, slam the door behind them and lock them up. Do that now, Mr Mosca, and then come back to the telephone.'

'Brilliant!' said Mosca, putting down the receiver. He turned to Octopus Scott and the others.

'Hurrah!' he said, his face glowing with pleasure. 'My friends, Herr Gustaffson has just given me the splendid news that our £15,000 is hidden in a drawer at the back of the strong-room.'

'Ours! Mine, you mean,' shouted Octopus Scott. He hurled himself on the lock of the door. 'A key! A combination key! A kingdom for a combination key!'

Mosca gave him one, and two minutes later he flung the door open. Lispington and Antonsson, who, on hearing somebody tampering with the lock, had thought that relief was near, suddenly saw a pack of villains swarm into the strong-room, shouting, cheering and laughing:

'Long live money!'

'Long live Herr Gustaffson!'

Octopus Scott was in the lead, blindly plunging right into the trap set by Agaton Sax and Julius Mosca.

Like a panther, Mosca the terrible was gathering his strength for the decisive leap. His wicked face was transformed by an expression of almost heavenly bliss as he watched the backs of his colleagues disappear into the strong-room.

Then he pounced. With one sweep of his arm he slammed the door and locked it. He had outwitted the lot. Now there was only one more to cope with . . . Herr Gustaffson. Mosca went to the telephone.

'Hallo, Herr Gustaffson. Well – that's that.'

'You've done it then?' said Herr Gustaffson (Agaton Sax, remember).

'Easily. It only took ten seconds,' boasted Mosca.

'Now I'm looking forward to a chat with you, Herr Gustaffson.'

'Splendid! At the moment I'm in a little room in the basement, very near the fire station, which occupies the greater part of the basement. In the next room, Smiling Sandra Smith is still counting the money – she counts each separate coin, so it will probably be some time before she's through. But if she tries to escape, I'll nab her. Come at once! You come in through the main entrance, turn left, down the stairs, follow the main corridor for about ten yards, then turn right into a narrow corridor. I'll be waiting for you there.'

'I'll be right over,' said Mosca, putting down the receiver, and dashing out of the room. He was shivering with anticipation and greed.

Agaton Sax rubbed his hands together and looked out of the window. He saw Julius Mosca come tearing out of the *Bykoping Post* building and head for the skyscraper.

Only a minute later Agaton Sax was standing in the corridor he had directed Mosca to. There is no need to tell you that Smiling Sandra Smith was not counting money in the basement at all. In fact that money was still in London, safely stored in the Bank of England.

Agaton Sax expected Mosca to be fully armed. He knew it would be his intention to take Herr Gustaffson by surprise and grab the money for himself.

He heard footsteps coming down the stairs towards him. It was Mosca. He came slowly and cautiously along the corridor, then stopped to listen. Agaton Sax got the impression he wasn't sure what to do next.

'Over here!' called Agaton Sax in Herr

Gustaffson's voice. 'I've just disarmed Smiling Sandra Smith and tied her up. Can you come straight in – the first door on the left? I can't leave, you see, because she's not to be trusted, as you know.'

'Fine. I'm coming.'

Mosca, of course, had no reason to think that Herr Gustaffson would try any tricks, why should he, since he had all the money?

Mosca stepped into the room. It was completely unfurnished, had no furniture of any kind, just bare, grey, concrete walls, still damp, since the building had only just been completed. At the other end of the room was another door.

'Here we are, I'm in the inner room,' shouted Agaton Sax.

'Good. I'm on my way.'

Mosca moved towards the farther door. He was on his guard, naturally, his right index finger caressing the trigger of his revolver. Suddenly he heard a sharp, metallic bang behind him. He jumped, spun round, and drew his revolver.

'Who's there?' he shouted.

'It is I, Agaton Sax!' The world-famous detective had resumed his own voice.

'Agaton Sax?'

'The very same.'

'Help!'

Not even Julius Mosca could help calling for help when he heard the terrible voice proclaiming that Agaton Sax was at his heels. Terrified and furious he threw himself against the door, but it was locked, and so was the other one. Julius Mosca was trapped.

Once more, Agaton Sax had demonstrated his marvellous skill as a ventriloquist and impersonator. He brushed a few specks of dust from his lapel, wiped his forehead with an exquisite silk handkerchief, and walked slowly to the stairs.

A terrible noise could be heard coming from the upper floors; angry and excited voices shouted wildly at each other, the sound of running feet echoed between the walls of the corridors, and panic seemed to be spreading like wildfire throughout the gigantic skyscraper.

'Agaton Sax! He's escaped! Help! We've got to get out of here! He's gone! Mosca's gone! Octopus Scott and Uncle Teetotum have gone! Where's the money? They've gone off with the money! Where's "Cauliflower" Charlie?'

These shouts were all coming from the villains who had been left in the skyscraper to guard Agaton Sax and the sleeping guests, waiters, and kitchen staff. They had become panic-stricken when three of them, including Smiling Sandra Smith, had discovered that the room in which Agaton Sax was held a prisoner was full of smoke but empty of Agaton Sax. Furthermore, they could hear banging and shouting coming from another room, whose door was firmly locked; nobody knew anything about a key to it.

Suddenly someone shouted:

'Run to the helicopters!'

'Yes, yes – to the helicopters!'

They rushed like madmen out of the building and piled into one of the cars parked outside.

'I'm the best driver,' said Smiling Sandra Smith, squeezing in behind the wheel, or rather squeezed in by all the others who came tumbling in after her, filling the front, and the back, and even clinging on to the boot, where they hung like great bunches of grapes.

Agaton Sax listened intently to the shouts and confused noises which reached him from all over the

building. There was only one thing to do, and he did it. There was a weapon that he had never tried before in his ceaseless war against crime. He decided to use it now. It was Bykoping's brand new diesel fire-engine, equipped with an extension ladder twenty yards long. Agaton Sax had advised the Fire Committee in all the details of its design and equipment before it had been ordered from the factory.

He raced into the garage, and jumped into the driver's seat. Half a minute later, he drove the fire-engine out into the street. Ahead he could see the rear of the car driven by Smiling Sandra Smith, travelling at terrific speed through the streets of Bykoping. Her yellow scarf was streaming in the wind like a tongue of flame. She was an awe-inspiring sight, callous, resolute, reckless – this was only her back view.

Agaton Sax knew exactly what to do. The fire-engine was of the best and most modern design available in Northern Europe, and Agaton Sax was definitely one of the most skilful drivers to be found in the same area. Furthermore, he was completely familiar with all the details of his machine. There was a triumphant smile on his lips as he pressed his foot down on the accelerator. Slowly but surely he was overhauling the other vehicle. The villains, panic-stricken, waved their arms, exhorting Smiling Sandra Smith to greater efforts.

'More gas, Sandra!'

'Step on it!'

'Who's following us?'

'Agaton Sax!'

'Help!'

'We're done for!'

But Smiling Sandra Smith only clenched her beautiful teeth, and clutched the wheel so hard that her nails turned white beneath their scarlet polish.

'Agaton Sax! Traitor! We'll fix him once and for all,' she growled, her foot pressed so hard on the accelerator that it was almost on the floor.

The two vehicles had now left Bykoping behind them and were heading south along the main road. Three miles ahead, on Johansson's meadow, the two helicopters were waiting for the villains.

Agaton Sax was now getting ready to deliver the knockout blow. The success of his plan would depend entirely on his presence of mind and the precision of his timing. At the point when the distance between them was 35 yards, the villains' car was travelling at 75 miles an hour, its maximum speed, taking into account the heavy load it was carrying, Agaton Sax increased his own speed to 110 miles an hour.

Petrified, the villains watched him getting nearer and nearer. He drew level with them, and Smiling Sandra Smith smiled no longer – she leant over the wheel, squeezing it, caressing it, urging it on in a sort of mad despair.

Then, suddenly, brutally, the hose was on them. The water hit them like an explosion, a headlong torrent, and it came so unexpectedly that none of them realised what had happened.

'We've gone into the lake!'

'Help! I can't swim!'

Water flooded them completely, it blinded them, made them grope desperately for something to hang on to. Only one of them had the presence of mind to act calmly; it was Smiling Sandra Smith, who reduced speed and finally drew up at the very edge of Johansson's meadow.

But she was too late. The water continued to engulf them, spurting in great jets from the hose that Agaton Sax had turned on.

'We surrender!'

'We're sinking!'

'All hands to the pumps!'

'Hand out the life-belts!'

'She's gone to the bottom!'

'Every man for himself!'

The crooks still thought they had ended up in a lake. With an elegant gesture Agaton Sax switched off the hose. Then he leant back and looked calmly at the villains, who, shivering and shaking, at last seemed to realise the awful truth.

The front door of the car opened, and Smiling Sandra Smith staggered out. She was soaked to the skin and her hair hung in rats' tails down her cheeks.

'You miserable cad!' she shouted. 'You've ruined my travelling-dress! I've got nothing else to wear – I don't travel around with a wardrobe, do I, you dirty rat. I'll sue you, you shabby, low-down little small-town swindler!'

Sobbing noisily, she flopped down by the side of the road. Agaton Sax was unmoved. Lighting a cigar, he said coldly:

'Get back into the car and drive it to the concrete tractor shed just beyond the next bend.'

The villains did as they were told. They wouldn't have dreamt of lifting a hand or even a finger against him. The door of the tractor shed was open. It was here that Agaton Sax kept his helicopter during the winter months.

'Inside!' he ordered. One minute later they were all safely locked up.

Puffing at his cigar, he looked thoughtfully at the lights of Bykoping, three miles away. It had been a hard day – hard but successful. All the villains were captured, all but one. Agaton Sax frowned. Only one – but a gang in himself. A feared and hated man, one of the most ruthless, scheming and intelligent gangsters to be named in the *Secret Code Register of Current Criminals*. Where was he? What was he planning at this very moment? What a disaster if he escaped now, when so much had been achieved.

'There's no time to lose,' he thought, hurrying back to the fire-engine.

Just as he was starting it up, he heard a voice behind him. It was a quiet, almost mild voice – yet threatening.

'Agaton Sax, I presume?' said the voice.

Agaton Sax gave a little start. He knew only too well the face he saw reflected in his rear mirror – it belonged to Herr Gustaffson.

'Yes, I am Agaton Sax,' he answered calmly.

'In that case, Mr Sax, I'm sorry to have to tell you that the game is up,' said Herr Gustaffson. He was invariably polite, but at the same time invariably menacing.

'So that's what you think, is it?' said Agaton Sax with a little smile.

'Yes. You cannot fail to have noticed, Mr Sax, that I'm carrying a revolver in my right hand.'

'Yes, I can see that.'

'I take it, therefore, that you will do as I tell you,' said Herr Gustaffson.

'Really?'

'Yes. You must be worth a ransom of some £1,930,000, and I need the money.'

'I see. As a matter of fact, I'm worth much more.'

'I'm not unreasonable, Mr Sax! Once I set my price I stick to it. But you must do as I tell you.'

'I know.'

'I'm sure you also know, Mr Sax, that I've been hidden here, behind you, all the time.'

'Of course.'

'I could hardly stop myself laughing out loud when you drenched that lot.'

'Is that so, Mr Gustaffson?'

'Yes. You are very clever and very efficient, Mr Sax.'

'Of course.'

'I do congratulate you, Mr Sax.'

'Thank you, Mr Gustaffson.'

'But we all meet our betters, even you, Mr Sax. All except me.'

'I'm afraid you're mistaken there, Mr Gustaffson.'

For the first time Herr Gustaffson looked uneasy. There was something in Agaton Sax's voice that aroused his suspicion. He looked round cautiously, and his finger pressed the trigger a little harder. But there didn't seem to be anything to worry about.

'Are you ready, Mr Sax?' he asked.

'Yes.' ('More so than you think!' Agaton Sax murmured to himself.)

'Good.'

How could Herr Gustaffson be such a fool as to believe that he was capable of outwitting Agaton Sax?

In the years to come, spent in the seclusion of his lonely cell, Herr Gustaffson put that question to himself, over and over again.

He became aware of his foolhardiness at the very moment he shot up into the air. He ascended vertically, at a terrific speed.

What had happened was that Herr Gustaffson had

been sitting, without realising it, on the light metal extension ladder designed by Agaton Sax himself. When folded it was so small that you could hardly see it. At the touch of a button, it would shoot some twenty yards into the air. Agaton Sax had touched the button.

'The game's up, Herr Gustaffson!' he called out.

'I acknowledge that I am *not* your superior,' Herr Gustaffson called back, politely raising his black bowler hat. He was clever enough to know at once when he was beaten.

'Hold on, Herr Gustaffson, I'm going to start the engine.'

'Thank you for telling me!' replied Herr Gustaffson.

As Agaton Sax drove his elevated prisoner back to Bykoping, he met the volunteer fire-brigade, who had already taken care of the rest of the gang. By this time a few of the Banquet guests had woken up, and were asking sleepily whether coffee would be served at the table or in the small side rooms.

Four firemen were detailed to look after Herr Gustaffson, who, with his usual politeness, thanked them for their attention.

Agaton Sax drove home. As he pulled up at the entrance he called out:

'Aunt Matilda! Is everything all right?'

'No, I've dropped several more stitches!' retorted Aunt Matilda.

'Stitches! What about the villains – and Antonsson and Lispington?'

'They're still in your room.'

He bounded up the stairs, flung open the door of his office, and shouted:

'Hallo! Are you there – Antonsson, Lispington?'

'Yes, we're here all right. And so is Mr MacSnuff.'

'Mr MacSnuff?' said Agaton Sax, pressing his ear close to the steel door of the strong-room. 'But surely, Mr MacSnuff can't be with you, Lispington?'

'Oh yes, he is,' said Lispington from the other side of the door. 'Mr MacSnuff was pushed in here some time ago by Julius Mosca. At first, I thought he was Octopus Scott, but then he said he was Mr MacSnuff, and I am quite satisfied that he is speaking the truth, because why should Mosca push Octopus Scott into the strong-room?'

'Don't believe him!' warned Agaton Sax, rushing to the window, and calling to the firemen who were waiting in the street below.

The fire-escape was raised to the window, and a fireman climbed up, ready with his extinguisher. Agaton Sax opened the steel door of the strong-room.

'Watch out, all of you!' he shouted.

Five seconds later, Lispington, Antonsson, and Agaton Sax had disarmed all the gangsters, including Octopus Scott. Gnashing his teeth, he realised that resistance was useless.

'The hour of revenge will come one day,' he threatened, shaking his fist at Agaton Sax. At that moment Mr Nick appeared in the doorway. Octopus Scott, who thought that Mr Nick was his hated enemy, Mosca, hurled himself violently at him. Lispington immediately rushed to Mr Nick's defence.

'Oh no, Mr Scott, you can't touch him! This one is *mine*. You are under arrest, Mr Mosca,' he said solemnly, placing his hand heavily on Mr Nick's shoulder.

This mistake was soon cleared up, and Mr Nick was once again given permission to put in a claim for the compensation due to him on each arrest.

By just before midnight, the Banquet guests were

alert and bright again, the real Swinging Susie and her group had been freed, the gang was securely locked up – the fire-engine was in its garage – and the table in Agaton Sax's editorial office was laid with coffee and cakes.

Agaton Sax's guests were Lispington, Antonsson, Mr Nick and Mr MacSnuff. They enjoyed a very pleasant chat until, just as Agaton Sax was filling his last pipe of the day, the wall called out:

'There's more trouble brewing, Agaton.'

'What on earth do you mean, Aunt Matilda?' said Agaton Sax. He was tired, and turned pale at the thought of anything else happening.

'Peterson's boy has just come in with a telegram for you, Agaton. It's from London.'

'Send him up, will you, Aunt?'

The boy gave the telegram to Agaton Sax, and, as usual when he brought a telegram from London, was given a sevenpenny tip. Agaton Sax glanced at the envelope.

'But this is not for me,' he exclaimed. 'It's for you, Mr Lispington.'

'For me?' said Lispington with a little shudder.

He tore open the telegram. A dark cloud passed over his long, anxious face.

'Dash it all,' he murmured. 'Confound it!'

'What's the matter? Trouble again?' said Agaton Sax, compassionately.

'Read it if you like,' said Lispington, handing the telegram to his Swedish friend.

Agaton Sax read:

CHIEF INSPECTOR LISPINGTON C/O AGATON SAX BYCROPMING OR BYKRPMNING SWEDEN STOP YOUR DOUBLE HAS BEEN SEEN LISPINGTON STOP WHAT ARE WE TO DO?

BRIGGS SCOTLAND YARD

More Beaver Books

We hope you have enjoyed this Beaver Book. Here are some of the other titles:

Agaton Sax and the Scotland Yard Mystery When Agaton Sax, ace detective from Sweden, is summoned to Scotland Yard to help recover the stolen Secret Code Register of Current Criminals, all kinds of hilarious and exciting adventures ensue! Written by Nils-Olof Franzén and wittily illustrated by Quentin Blake

Explore a Castle An exciting and original book which helps readers to work out how castles functioned and how people lived in them, including a special section on making a model castle of your own. Written by Brian Davison and illustrated throughout with black and white photographs and line drawings

Super Ghosts A Beaver original. Spine-chilling accounts of hauntings in all kinds of places, from churches to pubs, houses to village greens, and featuring haunted skulls, a vampire, poltergeists and even a ghost with a bad smell! Written by Mark Ronson

These and many other Beavers are available from your local bookshop or newsagent, or can be ordered direct from: Hamlyn Paperback Cash Sales, PO Box 11, Falmouth, Cornwall TR10 9EN. Send a cheque or postal order made payable to the Hamlyn Publishing Group, for the price of the book plus postage at the following rates:
UK: 45p for the first book, 20p for the second book, and 14p for each additional book ordered to a maximum charge of £1.63;
BFPO and Eire: 45p for the first book, 20p for the second book, plus 14p per copy for the next 7 books and thereafter 8p per book;
OVERSEAS: 75p for the first book and 21p for each extra book.

New Beavers are published every month and if you would like the *Beaver Bulletin*, a newsletter which tells you about new books and gives a complete list of titles and prices, send a large stamped addressed envelope to:

Beaver Bulletin
Arrow Books Limited
17–21 Conway Street
London W1P 6JD

9359308